FOREWARD

When I heard Tammy Revard, "The True Airhead," speak, I heard her conviction after all she has struggled through. Tammy had the courage to change her mindset and become an entrepreneur even though part of her brain is missing. When I first interacted with Tammy, she had such low self-esteem. After attending challenges and seeing the power of my mentoring, she broke through barriers and manifested a new mindset. She transformed herself into a confident entrepreneur. With all my years of experience, I value the importance of coaching and mentoring. This book will take you through her struggles and motivate you to take action and become a more confident individual.

Kevin Harrington

INTRODUCTION

Early in my life, I had many setbacks that resulted in me having low self-confidence. This made me feel insecure and resulted in such low self-esteem that I was not always making the best choices. Have you ever felt completely insecure or made bad choices like trying too hard to make relationships work because you thought you needed the security and stability? As I share my story with you, I will show you what I did to grow and learn so you can too!

But my life got worse before it got better. I became a literal airhead because of the brain injury I suffered. Yet this horrific trauma is what has ended up allowing me to help so many others. Maybe you have had something happen to you: divorce, low self-esteem, trying to be successful but getting nowhere, worried about what other people think of you, not doing things because that trigger in your brain says I can't do this because it won't be accepted by someone, or worried someone will make fun of you or not agree with your decisions.

As you read through the chapters, I will share with you what I learned and how I changed my mindset to overcome these challenges.

DEDICATIONS

This book is dedicated to my husband, Randy. He puts up with all of my airhead ways and lets me be myself. He can get negative at times, but when it comes to me, he is always supportive. Even with my wacky airhead ideas, including writing this book. Thank you to my family, especially my daughter, son-in-law, and my parents. I love you all so much; you may not like some of the things I say in here, but I had to speak my truth. The story would not be my true story if I fluffed it to make people look better. I know it's hard for you to understand that my emotions all come from love. Brain injury patients do get more emotional and cry more. It is hard for an outside person to understand when a brain injury survivor looks and acts normal. But inside, it is so hard to concentrate, function on a certain task, and not get emotional when hurt.

My closest friends, I consider you my other family/support system. My friends mean the world to me, and I truly cherish every friendship.

Willy Tubbs, thank you for calling me out in that life-changing speech, making me find my inner self and purpose. I would have never thought I could write a book until you broke through my barriers and challenged me to change. You instantly changed who I am just by that one question. "What do you have that is different from everyone else?" My answer, "I am a True Airhead."

Thank you, Dr. Breakthrough. Jimmy Ezzel, Gina Elson, Tsombawi Knibye Jr., Chef Katrina, and all of the Yep community.

Your positive support manifested me to become a confident entrepreneur.

A special thank you to Damien Nobel Andrews for meeting me in Los Angeles and doing a photo shoot out of the kindness of your heart. James Summerville, for all the time and patience you took to design my cover, and Mike Alden, for all your advice, respect, and knowledge; you have really helped me grow.

Thank you to Kevin Harrington, Natasha Grano, Mike Alden, James Summerville, Brittany Michalchuk, Brandon T Adams, Jesse Trevelow, Jeff the Entrepreneur, Mike Zeller, Coach Les, Hal Culbertson, and Tom Ziglar for all of your life-changing support and acceptance of my authentic self. All of you just wanted to help me, expecting nothing in return. You gave me life-changing self-confidence and changed my mindset forever. Words cannot express how thankful I am that you all chose to take me under your wings.

I never imagined watching Shark Tank that Kevin Harrington would write the forward of my book. Growing up reading Zig Ziglar's books, I would have never dreamed his son would help me write this introduction and support me in this book journey. When I was speaking on a platform with Tom, he took a picture of me and sent it to Kevin. Who could have fantasized this over 50 airhead with such low self-esteem that could not hold back tears when she went to speak would have two of the most respected people in the world guiding me. The biggest thing I pray everyone takes away from this book is to let go of their fear and anxiety and find a way to break through to their inner strength. I hope people find the courage to stop worrying about what others think of them. Once I let go of that, I increased my income and found a confidence within myself that would change who I was as a person forever.

TABLE OF CONTENTS

CHAPTER 1

GROWING UP

When I was born, the doctor was not at the hospital yet. The nurse kept telling my mother to hold on. Of course, my mother said she could not, and the nurse pushed me back up the canal. Who knows if that is part of the reason I slouched my whole life? But since I was a child, it was always pure pain to sit and stand up straight. That is not the whole reason for my brain damage because I was able to go on and lead a productive life until 2009 when I became the True Airhead, but we'll talk about that in a later chapter. According to both of my grandmothers, I was the apple of my parents' eyes until the day my sister was born. Both grandmothers would say to me, "You will always be my favorite grandchild for two reasons: one, because you were my first grandchild, and two, because I will never understand why your parents started treating you like you didn't exist once your sister was born." Do you know what it does to someone's self-esteem to be told that? I think both grandmothers cared for me and were trying to make me feel special. I just do not think they realized it would make me feel insecure. In their eyes, they truly believed they were making me feel special and loved. It is amazing how little words can change someone's path and affect them for years to come.

We had a motorhome, boat, and motorcycles. We camped every weekend. We had a group of families with kids close to our age that we would camp with every weekend. They were like family to us; we have years and years of childhood memories with them. I remember my sister begging to stay home one weekend because they never showed cartoons back then except on Saturdays, and she wanted to stay home and watch *Wonderama*. We would watch *The Brady Bunch* every day after school. I remember a few episodes of *The Flinstones* and *The Jetsons,* but other than that, we really did not watch cartoons.

I was a very good water skier but did not have good hand-eye coordination. I remember going to vision therapy as a kid. I was always the last one picked for sports teams and always dreaded when the teachers would let the kids pick the teams. No matter what, I was always last. I would stand there and just wish someone would pick me earlier. Teachers back then had no idea of the long-term effects of what bullying could do to someone's self-confidence and self-esteem. They allowed kids to be made fun of; I do not recall any time a teacher stopped kids from bullying others when I was in school.

My parents got divorced when I was twelve years old. My dad married a wonderful lady when I was sixteen. She had a son who was two months old when they started dating. My dad adopted him, and as far as I am concerned, he is my brother and always will be.

To clarify this now: my daughter asked that I not use our family's real names in this book. I know it makes it a little confusing and not as personal, but I am respecting her wish. We will call my dad and other mom (she hates the word step) "my parents," and my mom and her husband "my mom and her husband," so no names are mentioned.

My mom remarried when I was twenty-one. Her husband was a close family friend. His wife was a close friend of my mom's and had passed away when I was in college. She was only thirty-four when she passed. My mom's husband has two kids, a boy and a girl. I consider them my brother and sister as well. I have known them all their lives; I even started babysitting them when I was in junior high.

I had a very stable childhood. We lived in a wonderful neighborhood. My dad was an optometrist, and we lived so close to his office, he could walk to work. There were many kids in the neighborhood, and I am still friends with some of them to this day. My grandfather, Dad's dad, passed away from a brain tumor when I was ten years old. He had won many spelling bees as a kid, so the day of his funeral, I entered the spelling bee in honor of him. I thought for sure I would win, but that did not happen. I think I was knocked out in the fourth round. I can't even remember the word I was knocked out with.

After his death, we moved less than two miles away to a much nicer house that had a laundry room/apartment for my grandmother to move into. She had been crippled with arthritis since she was seventeen but still worked as a nurse for many years. Once we moved to the new neighborhood, my self-esteem took a hit. My sister and I changed schools, and the kids at this school were bullies. One minute, they would be my friends, and the next minute, they would talk behind my back and not include me in things. They would constantly make fun of me.

I remember the movie *Star Wars* was coming out, and a group of us were doing a dance based on it. Someone in the dance told me I should drop out because the girls were planning it, so when I fell to the ground as part of the dance, the audience would cheer. I just wanted to be on that stage and dance even though I was completely uncoordinated. To me, it was kind of like the movie *Shallow Hal.* I pictured myself as a beautiful dancer up there even though I probably looked uncoordinated and ridiculous. Sure enough, in the dance, when I was shot and fell to the ground, the whole school cheered. Maybe it was my age, but that did not hurt my self-esteem the way it may have years later when I thought back on it, but at that age, I just let things slid and did not care what others thought of me.

CHAPTER 2

JUNIOR HIGH

When I was going into junior high, they started busing for the LA Unified School District. Instead of the junior high I was supposed to go to in San Fernando Valley, I was chosen to be bussed to Watts. My mom started rallies and was all over the news trying to stop the bussing. It did not happen, so at the last minute, my parents and a group of neighbors enrolled us in a very small private school about fifteen minutes away. We carpooled every day with a group of other kids. Some children of celebrities went to that school, including Walt Disney's grandson and Ben Vereen's daughters. The school was very small. I think less than 150 students went, from kindergarten to twelfth grade.

This was right at the time my parents got divorced. My mom moved out, and we stayed with my dad. My mom had always been a homemaker and ended up starting a business to coordinate political dinners. This was in the 70s, when $50 a plate was considered an expensive event—nothing like today, where many start at $5,000 and go up from there.

Both my parents were very active within the community; my dad was president of both the chamber of commerce and the Kiwanis Club. They were both asked to run for political office and had friends that were in politics, but they never wanted to run. The reason we lived with my dad is they realized he could not afford child support and the private school.

My dad was great at driving a group of kids to school all the time in his Corvette. It could never be done today with the seatbelt laws, but we would fit three kids in the back little bubble behind the seats, and three kids would squeeze in the passenger seat, and he would drive us to school every other week. Four parents switched off in this carpool.

My dad kept the motorhome and got involved with our school snow ski club. Diane Disney, my dad, and two of the teachers would drive approximately twenty kids in our motorhome so we could spend the day snow skiing. It was so much fun. Again, in the 70s, the number of people squeezed into a car or motorhome was never an issue.

I had close friends in junior high and didn't feel like I was chasing popularity. I do remember always wanting to sing next to the microphone, but I was and still am tone-deaf, so the teachers did not want me there. No matter, I kept working my way up to the mic. To me, at that age, I just wanted to be on stage and sound good and get recognized for being popular. That was around the time the movie Grease came out. My friends and I would play that album over and over, and we knew every word to every song.

I went to the skating rink a lot and had a group of friends from there too. Because my dad worked full time and we still camped a lot on weekends, he would let my sister and I take the bus to the mall, pick out our clothes, and put them on hold. Then he would meet us when he got off work and say yes or no and buy them for us. It may have happened only once or twice, but I vividly remember that for some reason, especially a white OP short and top outfit with a Hawaiian print I got on one of these excursions. I don't know what ever happened to that short set, but I have never seen one as nice as it was; I am always looking.

My dad also let us take a bus to Santa Monica Beach when I was in junior high. I know the 70s times were a different time, but there is no way I would consider letting my daughter take a bus to the mall and beach with a friend even when she was in high school. That was around the times of the Hillside stranglers, and so many strange things were happening back then. In California, to this day, transportation like busses and subways is not popular like New York and other areas.

When my dad started dating my other mom, she started telling my dad he needed to get stricter. I was fourteen and already had freedom, and all of a sudden, this girlfriend came in and started saying, "No, you can't do that." I will never forget, one day, I had a date picking me up to take me to the roller rink. I had gone with him before, but my other mom made him come into the house and write down his driver's license info and his parents' phone number. I was so devastated and embarrassed that she would do this to me. Her attitude was, "If you are in a car accident, I am not going to answer the door and say I do not know if that is who you were in the car with." I want to be able to say you were with this person, and here is how to get a hold of his family.

She also would push, "Your reputation is so important." I think that is when I started worrying about what others thought of me; I did not want a bad reputation. I tried to stick to her philosophies, and years later, when I worked for the Ganz company, I found a mug and plaque with a poem on it that embodied her as a mother. I bought the mug and gave it to her.

I had the meanest mother in the whole world. While other kids had no breakfast, I had to have cereal, eggs, and toast. When others had pop and candy for lunch, I had to eat a sandwich. My mother insisted on knowing where we were at all times. You'd think we were on a chain gang. She had to know who our friends were and what we were doing. She insisted that if we said we'd

13

be gone for an hour, that we would be gone for one hour or less.

I am ashamed to admit it, but she actually had the nerve to break the child labor law. She made us wash the dishes, make beds, learn to cook, and all sorts of cruel things. I believe she lay awake nights thinking up mean things for us to do. She always insisted that we tell the truth, the whole truth, and nothing but the truth.

By the time we were teenagers, she was much wiser, and our lives became even more miserable. None of this tooting the horn of a car for us to come running. She embarrassed us to no end by making our dates and friends come to the door to get us.

My mother was a complete failure as a mother. None of us have ever been arrested or beaten a rap. Each of my brothers has served a mission and his country. And whom do we have to blame for this terrible way we turned out? You're right—our mean mother. Look at all the things we have missed. We never got to take part in a riot, burn draft cards, and a million and one other things that our friends did. She made us grow up into educated, honest adults. Using this as a background, I am trying to raise my children. I tell them to stand a little taller, and I am filled with pride when my children call me mean. You see, I thank God that He gave me the meanest mother in the whole world." (Orien Fifer, Phoenix Gazette)

This poem resonated with me so much, and I still have a mug with the saying on it. I keep it to remind me how special the love of a mother and child is, and every time my daughter said I was mean, I would think I was training her to be a respectful adult.

Chapter 3

High School & Junior Achievement and Where the Hustle Began

In tenth grade, I joined this amazing entrepreneurial club called Junior Achievement. High school kids had adult business advisors who would assign a product, and we had to go through the business process from start to finish. One year, our product was to sell street addresses. My job was to knock on people's doors and see if they wanted their address painted on the curb.

Then other members would do the painting with stencils. We won for the county that year and got to go onto the state convention.

Somehow, I ended up running for secretary of the state of California at that convention. I learned a lot at that convention. It was at a college campus, and I was in the library writing my speech, and a group of girls came up to me and said, "What are you doing?" I explained I was writing a speech, and they said, "Can we see it?" I said no, but they grabbed it from me. They read it, and then my opponent, who ended up as a newscaster for a major network, took everything I was saying and turned the speech against me. I was talking about ways we could grow Junior Achievement chapters. She went and talked about how I wanted to bring in the new and did not appreciate the existing members that were already there. My regret is that I should have talked about how she and her friends bullied and intimidated me. I was raised that you keep things positive and never would have thought to get on that stage and discuss the bullying. But over thirty years later, that still sticks with me. To this day, every time I see her do a report on TV, I think, "I hope karma got her and her friends." I do not believe she made it beyond a reporter, but she was with the national news for at least twenty-five to thirty years that I know of.

Another project we did in Junior Achievement was to make a ceramic fire hydrant to put fireplace matches in. My mom still keeps that by her fireplace. With Junior Achievement, I went to three national conventions and really learned a lot. There were classes on sales, leadership, marketing, and community unity.

In high school, because of the hustle I learned, I also sold Fuller Brush, a handheld sweeper, door to door after school. I would knock on the doors of homes by myself, and looking back, that could have been so dangerous. I would walk into people's houses by myself at sixteen and seventeen years old and show them the

18

products. With not a care in the world. No one was ever mean or made me feel uncomfortable.

When I turned sixteen, my Nana and Papa (grandparents from my mom's side) gave me two rolls of quarters and told me to always keep them in my car for emergencies. During high school, I had an amazing group of high school friends. To this day, we are super close and sometimes vacation together. I can go months without talking to them, and we always would pick right back up as if nothing has happened. I had been searching popularity and wanting a serious boyfriend all through high school. Thank goodness for my friends. I always loved doing things with them at school and on the weekends. I felt secure in many ways when I was around that group of friends. My friends were not mean girls; we never had arguments or falling outs that I can remember. My girlfriends and I would cruise Pacific Avenue. I would drive my mom's Chrysler Cordova with the sunroof open. Friends would get flowers and stand up, pretend we were in a parade, and wave at everyone. Or we would pull into the Burger King parking lot and wave for hours until midnight, and then go to the *Rocky Horror Picture Show.* One time, I even took my mom with us to the movie. She tried to be the cool mom to my friends.

I had a math teacher who really affected my life as well; he had us take a test where we figured out a number, and that was a grade. I went to him after class and said, "How can I be getting a D- in this class? I have not failed any test and turned in my homework." That teacher was so arrogant; he said, "I know my numbers are right. This is your grade." So I went to the principal in tears and switched to biology. After getting settled in biology class, we started dissecting frogs. Of course, lucky myself and lab partner got the only female and all the eggs. The math teacher came to me and stated he found three of my assignments in his notebook that he forgot to input, and would I please go back to his class. I said, "No, I am settled in biology and do not want to go back." I think that was junior year, but I had more than enough credits to graduate, so I did not take math for the rest of high school. Looking back again, just one teacher's words, the negativity and lack of empathy from that teacher affect my life for years to come. I will never understand how just some minor things can change people's course of life and path forever.

My girlfriends and I started dating college boys from the local fraternity for a few months on Friday nights. We would go to this restaurant at 7:00 p.m., get clam chowder, and stay in the restaurant. At 8:00 p.m., they started checking IDs, and it turned into a nightclub. One night, my friend's face dropped, and my mom walked in, sat at our table, and had a drink with us. My mom ordered a glass of wine. She seemed to have fun and never said a negative word about it. When we went back the next Friday, they made us leave and show the guards our IDs, which we did not have, of course. Well, years later, my mom told me she went back to the bar, showed them our pictures, and said, "They are seventeen. Drinking age is twenty-one. Do you want me to have you shut down?" But she never said a word to me about it.

In my senior year, bob haircuts became really popular. I had beautiful long hair and decided I wanted a bob cut. It looked so bad on me, like a bowl on top of my head. Of course, I had it cut a couple of days before prom. I had gone to many other dances but was not asked to prom. I wanted to go more than anything. My mom and her boyfriend thought it was funny, and they put a big sign on her motorhome saying, "Prom date needed here," and pointed it toward our house. They got a big laugh out of it, but I was made fun of for it so much. A bunch of the football players were at my neighbor's house, and all saw it. I was picked on so badly over it. I ended up having to get someone from Junior Achievement that went to another school to go to prom with me, and my mom paid for his tux so he would go. My hair looked so ridiculous, and my prom pictures were horrible.

I joined the Junior Miss contest. It was a contest broken into three parts. I believe you needed a 3.0-grade average to enter, but I could be wrong. They had a talent division, and I was such a good roller skater and wanted to do a skating routine to Queen's "We Are the Champions." My mom just could not see the vision and kept saying I couldn't go roller skate onstage. I look back now and wish I would have had the nerve to stand up for myself and do it my way because I was a good skater. A few years before, I had seen a tap routine someone did to "Mein Heir" from *Cabaret*. She had so much personality, and it was so cute. The lady from the pageant said I needed to sing it instead of dance it. Remember, I'm tone-deaf and can't sing for the life of me. I always dreamed of singing and wanted to, but there is no consistency in my voice. I know money was tight for my mom at the time, but she went and rented me a saloon girl costume. I look back now and think that song was about a hooker. I was so naïve; I just had no clue. This was a sweet and innocent pageant, and I was up there singing about being a hooker and had no clue that's what I was singing until years later. I'm sure I was last place in that contest.

I was also trophy queen at the speedway. Finally, I had my chance to be the beauty queen I had always wanted to be. My mom bought me this cute jumpsuit that was peach-and-gray striped. I went down to present the trophy, so excited, and the driver was a good-looking guy who was probably forty years old. All of a sudden, I felt so awkward having to kiss this older man. It was just a little peck, but it felt weird to me. Instead of letting loose and having fun, I was so concerned with what others thought. Look at it this way; it is way over 30 years later, and I am still looking at it like why did I worry so much about how people were going to judge me. I know that has stopped me from doing many things in my life, and it has taken me a long time to realize the ones who judge are insecure within themselves, and the ones who judge others have the issues and are unhappy within themselves.

I also ran a canned food drive that collected thousands of cans and won a couple of scholarships. I felt very stable in high school, mostly because of the support of my friends. I drove my mom crazy because it was hard for me to get to school on time every morning all through my school years. I always felt tired and had a hard time getting moving—and still do to this day. I still have brain fog, and mornings are hard for me. Looking back, I am not sure if I had fibromyalgia back then, but it even got to the point my mom would blast Pavarotti to try to get me moving in the mornings. There were many days I would miss the school bus, and she would have to drive me. It made her so frustrated. I have seen studies showing that teenagers that start school at 9 a.m. are much more successful. It is harder for many teenagers to get up so early and be at school by 7 a.m. like so many schools require. Physically, their bodies are meant to stay up later and sleep in. I know, for me personally, my days go better on mornings when I can sleep in.

CHAPTER 4
COLLEGE

I went to the Fashion Institute of Design & Merchandising in downtown Los Angeles, and I lived in a dorm down the street that was run by nuns. It was part of Saint Mary's College, and I guess the Von Trapp family from *The Sound of Music* stayed there when they were in Los Angeles. The day I moved in, I drove my Volkswagen bug filled to the brim from Northern California back to Los Angeles. Just as I brought the last load of my stuff up to the room, my college roommate arrived. She was an outgoing blonde from Wisconsin, bubbly and fun. She was not even there five minutes, and she said, "I've never been to the beach and always wanted to go." I said, "Come on," and we hopped in my car and went to Santa Monica Beach. We became instant friends and stayed friends all through college. I got a job working at the Hallmark store in the Fashion Mart, and I also started working at a company called Wendel Lighting in the mornings cold calling lighting companies at 6:00 a.m.—and I am so not a morning person. Then I also started to work at Wild Pair shoe store in the Santa Monica Mall. I don't know how I went to school and had three jobs, but I did. I got up every morning and was there on time, including the morning the Space Shuttle Columbia crashed. I remember my boss was so excited about watching it that he had us all take a break to see it. When it crashed, the whole office sat with tears in our eyes. My college roommate and I became little sisters for two USC fraternities, and we were living the life! We moved to an apartment near fraternity row, and we were able to get student tickets for all the football games, including the Rose Bowl. We enjoyed going to the football games and to parties every Thursday night at USC Fraternity Row. Through the years, I went to some fraternity events and still get yearly Christmas cards from one of my fraternity brothers.

Becky and I loved Fashion Institute, but it used to drive me crazy. I would study for two hours and get a B. My roommate would study for less than ten minutes and get an A. She was so much better at retaining things. We were both working on getting Merchandising/Marketing degrees. She was this beautiful blonde who did some modeling as well. She would pour salt on all her food, including pizza, so I came up with the idea of colored salt so people could see what they put on their food. This was in 1984 when things like that were not popular yet. My teacher gave me a C, which frustrated me so badly, saying that people do not want additional food coloring added to their food. Will you look at all of the colored salts you can find in your stores now. They are sold for margaritas, but I still wish I could take that product and say to that teacher, *"Hello, my idea made it to the marketplace, and you gave me a C."* My second product for that class consisted of pre-mixing Rum and Coke, so it was already made for convenience. Also so there was a controlled amount, so people at bars knew exactly how much they were drinking. I also got a C on that product. The teacher told me Coca-Cola would never want to associate their brand and name with an alcohol product. Their product was for families. I do not remember that teacher's name, but I wonder how many other students had great innovative products that he could not see the vision of? I wonder how many products he gave As to actually made it to the marketplace and were successful. I do believe he did kind of changed my mindset on some of my entrepreneurial visions. When I started college, I was coming off of Junior Achievement, wanting to be an entrepreneur. By the time I left college, I was in management training programs for retail stores and learning to work for others. I honestly believe that teacher took some of my entrepreneurial drive from me. I look back now and wonder, would my life had taken a different path if that teacher believed in my products and encouraged my talent?

My dream was to become a buyer for clothing stores or department stores. That is why I choose to go to Fashion Institute of Design and Merchandising. After I graduated and was managing clothing stores, I had the drive. I was the store manager for a clothing store named Susie Casuals at twenty years old. I found out it was taking buyers ten to fifteen years to work their way up to that position, and they only made $25,000 a year. I had way more visions for success than that. It took some time, but I decided that I needed to switch to sales, where I could make more money.

My college roommate and I learned an important lesson on money from a homeless lady we used to see on the public bus we rode from our apartment to Fashion Institute. This homeless lady's skin was so dirty it was actually peeling. We used to give her our spare change. We felt so sorry for her. Well, we went to eat at Mc Donald's one night, and this homeless lady went to pay; she had a paper bag that was filled with money. One of our other college friends just started yelling at her, saying, "We are so broke but always find ways to help you out, and you have enough money there to go live in a fancy hotel for months." We found out the nuns got a check from her brother and would cash it for her every month, but she chose to live on the streets even though she did not need to. She was happy living on the streets, and the money she had did not matter to her. Why she chose to live this way, I had no idea, and there were obviously some issues. To this day, it makes it hard for me to trust someone who walks up asking for money. In the back of my mind, I always think, are they legit? Do they really need money? Are they on drugs? I just have a tough time giving someone who walks up on the street money from that experience. Where my current husband looks at it as you do not know that could be Jesus giving you a test. He gives money to everyone who asks even if money is tight for us.

I had some wonderful times in high school and college and went on quite a few dates and had many boyfriends, but the relationships never lasted more than a few months. At that time in my life, all I wanted was a serious boyfriend. I worked hard, had friends with the girls, but something in my mind made me feel not whole because I was not in a real relationship.

CHAPTER 5

FINDING WHAT I THOUGHT WAS THE PERFECT MATE

I wanted a boyfriend so bad; I think I settled because I was in such desperation for someone to love me. I met a man who was an assistant manager of Leeds shoe store at Santa Monica Mall. I worked for Wild Pair, which was part of the same company, so we would share forms, etc. At that time, I did not have the confidence in myself to see all the bad warning signs in the relationship. He came from a family who truly loved him. He was an only child, and his mother and father spoiled him rotten.

His father was a complete neat freak, and his mother was a total hoarder. They actually never got married because his dad could not handle his mom's hoarding. However, his dad would come over every night to make dinner for his mom, they would get in an argument, and he would go back to his own apartment. They did this every night, and they truly did love each other, but their family was much different from the one I was raised in. The word *love* was used all the time in their house, and it was never used in mine. Even though they fought and argued constantly, they knew they loved each other and expressed it.

Eventually, he asked me to marry him. He gave me a fake cubic zirconia ring. His dad found an ad in the paper for it, and they were such tightwads, he bought it. To make matters worse, he embarrassed me so badly by making me take it to the jewelry store next door to Wild Pair to get it appraised. I guess he thought they would say it was a real diamond—but they didn't. I had to see these people every day, and I know they were laughing at me because my engagement ring was fake.

The funny part was, I was just so happy to have someone to be engaged to. I did not see the reality of the situation and what the future would bring. I never cared about name brands or needed anything super high-end, so it did not bother me at the time, but I look back now and think, "Why would I settle for someone who thought I was only worth a fake ring?" It took me many years to value myself and know my true worth.

Then his mother insisted I become Catholic. I was told I had to become a Catholic or I was not marrying her son. Of course, the man that would go by church and grab bulletins and lie to his parents about going to church went along with his mother. Again, another warning sign now that I'm older, but at the time, I just went along with it because I wanted a stable relationship so badly. So I went through all the classes to become a Catholic even though I did not believe in some of the things the Catholic church did. For instance, going up for communion; if people feel they have sinned, they do not go up to receive the communion. So some people in the church would stare at others who do not go up as, *"Oh, they have done something they are not supposed to."* Again, being an insecure person at the time, I was so worried about what other people would think if I do not go up that I would go receive communion no matter what. I was not allowed to receive communion before I completed all the classes. In my opinion, that was so wrong. Here, the priest would talk about how welcoming the church is, but then, they say, "You are not welcome because you are not one of us." Maybe it is just me. They feel you need to earn it, but it bothered me that they were not welcoming like they said, and certain people were so judgmental.

We had a very lovely wedding on August 8, 1987. We got married at Saint Monica's Church in Santa Monica and had the reception in my parents' back yard.

The wedding was wonderful, and my family was so supportive. We had well over 100 people, and it was beautiful. My husband and I went on a three-day cruise for our honeymoon. I was so thankful to be able to go, even if for just three days. We had a very nice time, and when we got back, he moved into my apartment.

That's when I really started learning what a tightwad he was. We did not have a barbeque, and we were having friends over for dinner the next weekend, so I bought a little portable barbecue for $5.99. He yelled at me for two days straight for spending that $5.99. Unfortunately, that did not make me want to stop spending money—it did just the opposite to me. I was in debt for many years because I was constantly buying things for comfort or impulsive reasons. Then I donated some clothes to the neighbor, and he actually had the nerve to go knock on his door and ask for them back.

We lived in two apartments before we bought our first house the year after we got married. At this time, his dad passed from a brain tumor. We spent a lot of time with him before he passed. My favorite memory was that he kept getting upset because he thought the nurses were putting lit cigarettes in his bed, and he was afraid it would catch on fire. It was really the blood pulse machine they had attached to his finger, which had a red light on it. We would have to explain every day that it was okay. It was funny and a good memory of such a fun time. He did not believe in life support and was just ready to go to the Lord. While my husband's mom believed in a life was a life and keep supporting, no matter what anyone felt. He put my husband in charge of everything because he did not want life support. It was such a battle with his mom; she started begging the doctors to put him on life support against his wishes. The doctors called us in and asked us to put him on life support, and my husband said, "Absolutely not."

The doctors were completely on his mother's side; it was

so uncomfortable. He stuck to his guns, gave his dad his wish, and his dad passed away in peace. It was very difficult, but we got through it.

Then my grandma, Dad's mom, got very ill. Our family camped out at the hospital for days. That was when the handheld Nintendo Gameboys came out, and we played a lot of games while spending time with her. The last night, it was just my other mom and me on each side of the bed. We were both so tired we were falling asleep. I was half asleep, and my grandma let go of my hand. I looked over, and she had stopped breathing. She had been in a lot of pain but went in complete peace. I loved her so much it was wonderful to know she was no longer in pain, but she will always have a place in my heart.

My husband and I struggled back and forth with a few jobs until I got pregnant in 1991. It was not planned. I took birth control, but we had been married almost five years, and we were ready.

CHAPTER 6

BIRTH TO FIRST FEW YEARS OF MY DAUGHTER

I had a very high-risk pregnancy. To start, my alpha-fetoprotein (AFP) was supposed to be 2 percent, and mine was 4.6 percent, so they thought my daughter could have spina bifida. We had to go through a lot of genetic testing, and they actually figured out one of her 13th chromosomes was attached to the 14th, but it ran in my husband's family, so they were not as concerned. I was having to keep track of all my kicks and going for checkups weekly. Once, I was going to the movies with a friend and said, "I must go to the hospital for my checkup first. It will just take ten minutes." I am so glad I took her with me that day because I walked in for my basic test, and my blood pressure was too high. I have always had low blood pressure. They hospitalized me and got a hold of my husband. His response was, "Since her friend is there, I do not need to go to the hospital." It hurt me so bad that here I am in the hospital being monitored, terrified I could lose this baby, and he stayed at work. I was hospitalized twice due to toxemia, and the second time they told me to go home and get diapers and whatever I needed for the baby, as she would probably be coming early. Well, that was in September 1991, and my daughter was not born until November. I finally got an appointment to be induced on my grandmother's birthday. I was so excited she was going to carry on her legacy. The day before was the opening of the Ronald Regan Library, and Presidents Ford, Carter, Bush, Nixon, and Regan were there. We were so excited that was going to be the newspaper of the day she was born. I was packing up to go to the hospital, and they called saying there was a baby who was breach and they had to move my inducement two days. I was so disappointed because that baby girl was not going to be born on my grandma's birthday. It just was not meant to be.

The day my daughter was born was the day Magic Johnson announced he had AIDS. To this day, I still see the videos with Magic Johnson talking with that date stamped November 7, 1991 at the bottom. My daughter was born completely healthy with no issues at all. My husband and I took a class about singing to the baby and that it keeps them calm and relaxed. Both of my husbands have good singing voices. My first husband sang to my daughter this song we made up through the entire birthing process. It is so hard for me not to say names in this book, but I am respecting my daughter's wishes. So instead of her name, which flowed with the song for this book, I will

42

just write "my daughter." The words to the song were this: "My daughter, baby, I never knew I could love anybody as much as I love you. You are the sunshine that brightens my day, my daughter, baby, I love you always." Her father sang that song over and over while she was being born from a cassette tape we brought to the hospital. They said there was too much protein in my placenta, and that is what caused such a high AFP. They made me sign papers and took my placenta for research. My whole family was there for my daughter's birth and was so supportive. We were all what I thought was a close family then.

This sounds strange because I'm respecting my daughter's wishes not to use names, but my Nana (Mom's mom) asked me to name my daughter a particular name. I said, "As long as you don't call her the nickname to it." I knew a girl in school with that nickname, who was a bully. Sure enough, weeks after my Nana passed, my mom and sister started calling her the name I asked her not to be called and telling her she should change her name to that

43

nickname. It bothered me so badly because that name was chosen at my grandmother's request, and my mom and sister knew I could not stand her being called that nickname. I honestly believed they started calling her that because they knew I did not want that. It bothered me so bad they would do this; they knew my request not to call her that. They would purposely call her that loudly in front of me. To this day, it makes me sick to my stomach every time my mom and sister call her that. Then, after I got divorced and she got married, she legally changed her name to my ex-husband's last name. He begged her to do it to carry on the name. Again, it was just another manipulation against me because my ex knew how bothered I was by her not carrying on the name my Nana choose for her. Part of the reason it bothers me so bad is it meant so much to Nana to be able to name her.

Money was very tight, but her dad insisted I be a stay-at-home mom. His mother worked all his life, and he felt it was important that I be there with her.

When my daughter was nine months old, her dad got accepted to the California Highway Patrol (CHP) academy. So I raised her on my own when she was an infant while her dad was up in Sacramento for training.

Right before his graduation, the LA riots broke out. My husband drove police cars as needed, from Sacramento to Los Angeles, but he was not allowed to be on the front lines because he had not graduated yet. It was great for our little family because he got to come home and spend a couple of days with us at such a scary time. One of the recruits' brother had a plane, and they flew back to the academy in Sacramento. He graduated from the Highway Patrol Academy by the skin of his teeth, but he ended up not making the probation period. That's when I realized I had to go back to work.

He went back to his old job and started applying for other police departments. I started working at a preschool so I could be with my daughter every day.

During my first week at the preschool, I met some reserve officers that worked full time for a Grocery Chain Security Department. I told them about my husband and got him an interview, and he ended up getting hired at the Grocery Chain Corporate Office and becoming a Reserve Police.

Life was good until one night when we went to the local grocery store, and my daughter was in the cart with her dad pushing it. I went to grab an item, and this man walked up and said, "Officer, do you remember you arrested me?" My husband said, "Yes," and the man said, "I want to thank you. My life was going down the wrong path. You woke me up, and I am doing great now. I needed that wake-up call." Instead of taking that positively, as I saw it, my husband became an on-guard, different person. His attitude was that man could have pulled out a gun and shot his daughter or him. He carried a backpack with a gun everywhere we went. I kept begging him when we would go to a friend's house, "Please do not bring it. There will be a group of kids there." But he always had to have it.

Thank goodness no one ever got hurt, but his attitude toward life, and toward me, was never the same. He always was and stayed a great father to my daughter, but he never treated me the same.

Around the same time, my bank account got drained. Someone that worked for the check company made checks with our account number and cashed them. I went to get gas, and my ATM card would not work. Thank goodness I had the $20 from my Nana and Papa in my glove box. I called my dad and explained, and his words were, "That's a life lesson. You should always keep cash for an emergency." So many of my friends had their parents help them financially for so many things, but this was not even in my control, and I was still denied money to get through the weekend. My mom said no also. My Nana and Papa wired me $100, and I gave it back to them the next time I saw them.

Our life was good overall at this time. We had so much love for my daughter and spoiled her rotten. We would go camping with my family on vacations and were involved with our church.

When my daughter went to kindergarten, my parents did help us and paid for her to go to Catholic school for two years. We got involved with the church and made many friendships there. I thought her dad and I had the perfect relationship until he cheated on me with my best friend and ruined the friendship. The friend's husband called me and said that their friend saw them making out. I did not know until years later that her husband had confronted mine. I do not know why I've always had the attitude of, "If you want to cheat, go ahead as long as you come home to me every night." I tried for years to remain friends with the friend, but her husband did not want her around me. Every few years, we would get together and have fun again, but we were never super close like we had been. It was sad because we were so close and always had fun even when we went a year without seeing each other and would get back together. We would just pick right back up, but the friendship will never be the same.

CHAPTER 7

MY DAUGHTER'S
EARLY YEARS AND WHEN
I GOT FIBROMYALGIA

While working at the preschool, I got chickenpox. It was so bad my husband heard the doctors in the hallway arguing over what they should do with me. One wanted to keep me, and the other said no, I needed to be quarantined. I got sent home, but that year, I kept getting sick. I got my wisdom teeth pulled out, stood up, and passed out. My husband had to take me to my parents so they could take care of me because I had this young child, and I couldn't care for her while he was at work. I am so grateful because they took really good care of me while I regained my strength.

We decided to have Thanksgiving at our house that year, and Nana said she and Papa would come out a day early and help me, but not to tell the rest of the family. So Nana and Papa came out, and we made the best dinner. She joked about punching pies, but she would not allow me to tell the family she was there. Then months later, my mom asked her something about staying at my house, and she said, "The first night." My mom said, "The first night you stayed and helped her cook?" She had to admit it. I look at it now and think that maybe part of the reason my mom is so secretive and avoids things is that it was passed on to her from her mom. I don't know if it's impulse from the brain damage, but unlike my family, I'm an upfront, tell-it-like-it-is person. I don't like lies and secrets. It's gotten me in a lot of arguments through the years, but I would rather deal with things and figure them out than avoid them and talk behind backs. It really bothers me when people talk behind my back rather than come and discuss it.

My daughter started dance lessons and fell in love with it. At three years old, they moved her up to the ten-year-old class because she was a better dancer than everyone else. She has great rhythm, the opposite of me, thank goodness. She danced with a little boy to songs from *Grease* and *Dirty Dancing*, and they even won a State Championship. They were so good. She even danced in college, and she is a great dancer to this day.

My nephew was born in September. Like my family was there for my daughter, we were there for my nephew. I had interviewed for a sales rep job and gotten hired with Ganz, a giftware company, that weekend. I had been all open arms with my daughter, letting my family take her whenever they wanted, but the same was not true for my sister and her son. After my sister had my nephew, my mom dropped us off at my sister's house to see the baby. My sister and her husband were home and knew we didn't have our car with us but locked us out and wouldn't answer the door or let us see the baby. So we were stuck with a four-year-old and no car. That is just the kind of treatment I have gotten from my sister most of my life.

I got sick again that year. This time, I had meningitis. They did a spinal tap and sent me home. Shortly after, I got the most massive headache and went back to the hospital. They did an ultrasound, and my spinal fluid had leaked out. They did a blood patch, but after that, and to this day, I have had a groggy feeling. I also have had to have occipital nerve blocks because I started to get such painful headaches, and I was diagnosed with fibromyalgia. Ever since then, I have had a feeling that I can only describe as feeling like you have a bowling ball on your head all the time. It is impossible to explain what it feels like to be groggy all the time, but I always feel like I could easily just go lie down and take a nap. When I am tired, it gets worse. A couple of months later, we were up in Big Bear, and my grandma, my other mom's mom, was doing some kind of art project where she had a blender going for what seemed like ten minutes. It caused me so much pain. I got to the point I couldn't handle it, and I asked her to please turn it off. The family got mad at me, saying I was over-dramatizing. I left so upset. It may have been a Thanksgiving because that Christmas, I was told I was not invited. I was so hurt. My other mom has had Epstein-Barr, and it was okay for her to be in bed for a couple of days at a time, but if I am sick, I'm faking it in my dad's and her eyes. I do understand it is hard to see how much pain a person with a chronic illness or brain injury is in when it is not visible to the human eye. My biggest issue with my family is the lack of respect they have for me; they think I fake it for attention. I wish for one day they could sit and listen to that blender going full force with the grogginess and pain I have in my head daily.

When Christmas Day rolled around that year, my other mom called in tears, and we ended up seeing them that afternoon. They will never understand how much it hurts my self-esteem every time they make me feel unwelcome. They get upset with me for getting emotional but will never understand how it feels to be in pain all the time. My body still aches at times from the fibromyalgia, especially on overcast or rainy days, and my muscles are so bad at every pressure point. People just don't understand that when you feel this way, you are always on the brink of tears, and something that seems small to them can easily be so overwhelming emotional, especially when your head is pounding. Once the tears start, for most brain injury patients, they are very hard to control and stop. I cry when I get compliments too. It is just an emotional sensor I can not stop.

CHAPTER 8

FINDING MYSELF

I started working full-time for Ganz right after my daughter started pre-K. I had a fantastic boss who I am still friends with all of these years later.

Ganz was a gift wear company that had over 1500 gift wear items. We sold Teddy Bears, Picture Frames, and so many other knick-knack items that were so popular then. I worked for them for seven years. It was really fun selling those items, but there were many tough days as well. Back at that time, knick-knacks were so popular. I built relationships with customers, and they really trusted me. I was still groggy, and getting up in the mornings, getting my daughter to school, and then work was hard for me. I was far from the perfect housekeeper because I was so tired all the time.

I remember one time I had gotten a new manager; the manager I was so close to had taken a leave. The new manager went on a call with me and said, "I have never seen someone sell the way you do. You have built friendships with these clients, and they trust your word. You put in a little aggressiveness when you know that a product is proven, but overall, you have such a soft approach to your selling." Well, I am jumping ahead right now, but in Network Marketing, they say all the time the best way to sell is to get your potential clients to know, like, and trust you. I am so good at building relationships in person. I am great at communicating and getting to know people, but over the internet, when my spelling and grammar are not as good, it is harder for me to keep the inbox going. I am a very upfront person and like to tell it like it is. I would never want to sell anyone anything I did not believe in. Sometimes, I overthink sales, but if I do not have conviction of belief for the product, I ethically do not feel comfortable selling something I do not believe in.

A few years later, I started selling Yellow Page ads to try to make more money, and it was hard for me to balance life. I worked for two different yellow page companies. I worked hard, put in so many hours, and I was successful. I was number one in new accounts at Yellowbook and won Rookie of the year at Verizon. I did settle chasing after smaller accounts because I knew many others were going after the big fish. So my sales were not as high as those of others, but I had consistency. I still worked on the award shows part-time while I was selling Yellowpages. There were ups and downs, but life overall was good. Working in sales is not always easy. Yellowpages really taught me to adapt to all types of business. There were days I would sit in my car in front of an account and have to force myself to get out of my car. Or motivate myself to believe I was not going to be rejected. I would envision my future and was successful, but with anyone in sales, you are only as good as your next sale, so you are always up and down. So many reps would only work eight to four. I found out I closed quite a few sales around six at night, catching the owners at the businesses when they were ready to close their doors. When I started with Yellowpages, the internet was not popular yet, so it was truly making a difference in businesses. People would call and say, "I know the book came out." My phone started ringing more.

CHAPTER 9

WORKING AWARD
SHOWS SOMETHING
I TRULY LOVE DOING

When my daughter was in kindergarten, she became best friends with a girl whose mom was a talent coordinator for award shows, including the American Music Awards, Billboard, and many others. I was so intrigued by what she did. It is sad, but I honestly do not remember the first show I attended. It is so frustrating that I cannot remember my first experience, but from that point until now, twenty-four years later, I have worked on these shows, and I hope to keep being able to do them. With COVID, there is no audience department right now, which is my department now. Once, I attended one and started getting invited to work on them. I was in absolute heaven. I am going on 24 years now, so I have worked on Oscars, Grammys, Emmys, Superbowl halftime shows, many MTV shows, including the Superbowl halftime show, and so much more.

I remember my first talent escort job. I was assigned to LeAnn Rimes. She was only thirteen years old, and her parents were still working, so her mom's friend was her chaperone. For some amazing reason, I really clicked with her and the band that day. Years later, she performed at a concert at a park I went to, and she waved at me three or four times during the concert. This was at least fifteen years later. After the concert, the people I was with wanted to hang by the gate. I was so embarrassed because working the award shows, we are never fans. Well, she came out to the gate and came straight to me and said, "It's been bugging me all night. Where do I know you from?" I told her I was her first talent escort at the American Music Awards when she was thirteen. She said, "Of course! I kept waving at you because I knew I met you before." I have had twenty-three years of experiences like this and have seen and met so many celebrities.

I worked on many Billboard Music Awards and had so many great experiences. There were years I worked in the talent department. One year, I was in charge of getting all the celebrities from a back hallway to a limo so they could drive up to the red carpet. I got a list of what names and room numbers each celebrity was checked in as. The names some of them were checked in as were a riot like Victoria Secret, Jack Daniels, Ima Rockstar. Barry Williams, aka Greg Brady, did a comedy song to Slim Shady singing he was Greg Brady. When he came down to the registration desk, he started singing the song

Tammy to me. I just thanked him, but I look back and wish I would have had more personality instead of being so embarrassed when he sang to me. I do not know why I did not tell him how much I loved the Brady Bunch as a kid. Or pretend to be all excited to see Greg Brady. Instead, I just let him sing to me and smiled and said thank you. There were many Billboards I got to work in the pit. It was amazing to be right upfront with some of the most amazing singers in the world. From popular ones in today's times to singers I grew up listening to that my parents always played like Neil Diamond, Cher, Bette Midler to my favorite classic rock bands and Garth Brooks, another favorite of mine. One of my favorite all-time Billboard experiences was when I walked into a dress rehearsal, and they were doing a tribute to Aerosmith. I looked up on the screen, and there was my daughter when she was about six years old carrying a star she made that said "Aerosmith Rocks." The clip was from the Kids Choice Awards many years before. Here was my daughter in this Billboard Tribute years later. It was so special to see her on the screen and part of a tribute with one of my favorite bands. I believe this was years after I saw him at the Super Bowl, but I honestly do not remember years anymore.

Another favorite I will never forget was Steven Tyler. I sat next to him at the American Music Awards, and two weeks later, I was in Tampa as the audience coordinator of the Super Bowl halftime show. We had 4,000 eighteen- to thirty-five-year-olds who were going to run onto the field after NSYNC. That was before the internet was really big, and we had to go to college campuses and malls to recruit. I was the very first bus to go and the first one to walk out, with 750 kids. At rehearsal, I walked my busload of kids into our tunnel. It was cold outside, but with all those kids in the tunnel, it was so hot in there. We had to be in the tunnel for over an hour by the time they got everything arranged. I will never forget this young blonde, blue-eyed high school student who asked me, "Is Steven Tyler really going to be there, or do they have stand-ins?" He was faced toward the field. I could see Steven was starting to walk from the other end of the tunnel in a black trench coat, and Joe Perry was behind him. I will never forget that kid's eyes when I said, "If you can be really quiet, turn around." His blue eyes just lit up with pure joy and amazement. By that time, people were noticing and yelling, and they had the crew grab each other's hands and make a chain to hold everyone back. The blonde young man was behind me, and as Steven was walking, he saw me, turned around, gave me a kiss on the cheek, and said, "Hey, California girl, you're in the wrong state." The young man was like, "OMG, you know Steven Tyler?" I said, "Not really. I just sat near him at an award show two weeks ago." He went around and told all these people I was friends with Steven Tyler, and a couple of girls came up and asked if I would introduce them to Steven. Of course, I said, "No, I don't really know him."

One of my top ten life regrets was the following year's Superbowl in New Orleans; my grandma's neighbor across the street worked for the Rams. The next year, the Super Bowl was in New Orleans. We were not working the halftime show but working some pre and post-shows. My grandmother's neighbor said she could get us tickets in the owner's section for $350 each. My husband said, "No, we were on the field last year. I'm not paying $700 to sit in the stands." I should have gone behind his back and just bought them. He would get so angry, and I was too scared to go against him. Of course, he changed his mind once we got to New Orleans, but it was way too late then, so we watched the Superbowl in a hotel room 711 with a bunch of other MTV staff instead of being there in those great seats. It was a fun experience, but I wish I would have just spent the money and gone to that Superbowl!

Here is a blog I wrote about working a Superbowl halftime show.

1. Working A Superbowl Halftime Show

Have you ever thought, wow, the music just does not sound great at a halftime show concert? Well, here is my experience working the 2001 Superbowl halftime show, and hopefully, it will teach you something you never thought about from an inside perspective. For me, the 2001 Superbowl will be a day/night I will never forget. A group of us spent two weeks in Tampa recruiting to get 4,000 18-25 years olds for the field. We meet Sunday afternoon at a high school, and I was on the first bus out of 80. It was like a parade; people stood outside their homes waving us on. We got to the stadium, and they handed us these pink field pass necklaces we could not keep. Some big drunk guy tried to pull my pass off of me, and I had to yell for security as I walked into the stadium with the kids behind me. We got into the tunnel. It was cold outside but sweaty and hot in the tunnel with 750 of us. They started to bring the stage out. They only have two and a half minutes to get it to the field and secured into place. It was amazing to see over 100 people carry the stage and sit underneath it. They get danced on, have to listen to loud music and sound vibrations while they are sitting underneath for the entire halftime show. Back in the tunnel, my crew had to make a chain as Brittany Spears, Nelly, Missy Elliott, and Aerosmith walked by. The reason for the chain of hands was to hold the kids back. As Steven Tyler walked by, he saw me and kissed me on the cheek and said, "California girl, you're in the wrong state" at the rehearsal two nights before.

Superbowl night, he just waved at me when he walked by. We ran with the kids onto the field. All these white lights flashed; it took me a few seconds to realize those were camera flashes. I was assigned to stay towards the back by my tunnel in case there were issues, so I ended up standing and dancing with Brittney Spears' mom. Once the show ended, there were seven kids that were left when the football players started running out. I was told we needed to stay on the side of the field to keep those kids safe. Darn, the luck; just kidding. Lucky us got to stand to the side and watch a few seconds of the second quarter before I had permission to take them to the bus. I was the only crew member who got to stay with some MTV executives. The experience gave me a lifetime memory I am so grateful for. I've been so blessed getting to do some things very few people in the world have experienced.

What people do not realize is all comes from hard work. I would never have been in that position and get to do the things I did if I did not work hard and apply myself. Enjoy the Superbowl today but think of all the people working behind the scenes, sitting under the stage, etc. You probably didn't even realize that to put that stage up in two minutes is a big reason the sound is not the same as a regular concert where they spend hours getting the sound. Right!

Think of them bent down and having to feel the pounding of dancing feet. We all have amazing experiences in life, but sometimes we need to look at the whole picture instead of complaining about the way something looks or sounds. It is an amazing thing they can put that show together and get the stage taken down between the game.

Many of the shows I worked on were with MTV. I worked on many MTV Spring Breaks, Beach Houses, Summer in the Keys, VMA's Movie Awards, etc. One of my best memories was working on the famous MTV

Spring Breaks in Cancun, Mexico. We wanted 18 to 25-year-olds and would walk along the beaches and go to the bars to invite kids to come. Drinks were not allowed inside the performance area, and it would get very hot in the sun. So we were constantly switching audience members inside and outside all day long. We started filming early in the morning because of the heat. We would arrive at 6 a.m., and there would be lines of college kids that stayed up all night and were ready for the filming. They usually would only last an hour or two unless we had some special band booked. It was a pretty fun experience, though. I personally loved every minute no matter how tired I was because we would go to the bars and recruit late in the evenings and then work in the heat all day long, but I would also check people in, dance, and help with the audience. On one of the trips to Cancun, I stayed an extra day and went swimming with the dolphins. That was such a amazing experience. I was so good at waterskiing that I was able to stand up like I was skiing when the dolphins pushed on my feet. I absolutely loved every second of it. I bought the video because it was such a neat experience. My other mom enjoyed my video so much that she planned a trip with her girlfriends and went swimming with the dolphins too.

I worked on many Billboard Music Awards and had so many great experiences. There were years I worked in the talent department. One year, I was in charge of getting all the celebrities from a back hallway in the hotel to a limo so they could drive up to the red carpet. I got a list of what names and room numbers each celebrity was checked in as. The names some of them were checked in as were a riot like Victoria Secret, Jack Daniels, Ima Rockstar. Barry Williams, aka Greg Brady, did a comedy song to Slim Shady singing he was Greg Brady. When he came down to the registration desk, he started singing the song Tammy to me. I just thanked him, but I look back and wish I would have had more personality instead of being so embarrassed when he sang to me. I do not know why I did not tell him how much I loved the Brady Bunch as a kid. Or pretend to be all excited to see Greg Brady. Instead, I just let him sing to me and smiled and said thank you. There were many Billboards I got to work in the pit. It was amazing to be right upfront with some of the most amazing singers in the world. From popular ones in today's times to singers I grew up listening to that my parents always played like Neil Diamond, Cher, Bette Midler to my favorite classic rock bands and Garth Brooks, another favorite of mine. One of my favorite all-time Billboard experiences was when I walked into a dress rehearsal, and they were doing a tribute to Aerosmith. I looked up on the screen, and there was my daughter when she was about six years old carrying a star she made that said "Aerosmith Rocks." The clip was from the Kids Choice Awards many years before. Here was my daughter in this Billboard Tribute years later. It was so special to see her on the screen and part of a tribute with one of my favorite bands. I believe this was years after I saw him at the Super Bowl, but I honestly do not remember years anymore. Then, years later, I took a group of girlfriends to American Idol Rehearsal. There were eight of us that day. That was the year Steven Tyler was a judge on American Idol. We were set in the middle section about four rows up. I was at the end of the row. Steven came over, sat down next to me, and put his arm around me. He started asking me what I thought about the contestants, and I got the nerve to tell him how excited the boy was at the Super Bowl halftime show. He looked right at me and said, "I remember seeing you in the tunnel, and I have seen you at other shows too. Weren't you at the MTV Aerosmith Icon?" I said, "Yes, I was," then my old boss, who was sitting next to me, said, "That's so cool. Do you remember when we were in Vegas and had to sit in a Limo because you wanted to switch hotels?" Now she did sit with him for a couple of hours when she was assigned to him. I was never with him for more than two minutes at a time, but working seat fillers, I do walk past the talent a lot as they're sitting in their seats during commercial breaks. He said, "Honey, was that more than eight years ago?" She said, "Yes." He said, "I'm sorry. I was not clean and sober then. I do not remember." Then he said to me, "I think I saw you at a Grammy as well." A girl behind tapped him to ask a question. I looked over at my friend, and Oh my God, with his arm still around me, he grabbed my boob. Again, another situation in which I was so shocked, I just acted like nothing happened. He then said to me, "When is your birthday?" I said, "July 2nd." He said, "No, that's not it. I don't know what it is, but we have a connection. I know I will see you again." He gave me a kiss on the cheek and walked away. I was so shocked he had grabbed my boob. Later, I said, "I guess I should have asked for concert tickets as a joke." I was really surprised he did that, but I guess because I respect his singing so much, I did not have the nerve to say anything or know the right words to say. I did see him again at a Grammy, and he came up to me and said, "Where is Smoky?" I did not have a run down like I normally carry. Music was playing loud. Airhead me said, "Do you need to go outside to smoke?" He had this young publicist with him that said, "No, he does not want to go smoke. He is looking for Smoky Robinson." I said, "Sorry, let me go find someone from the talent department for you." I bumped a seat filler in the back so he could stay seated near where he was going to present and got a talent person to take care of him. That is the last time I have seen Steven Tyler. I have no idea why I have so many stories and connections about him than all the other celebrities in the industry.

Again, with over twenty years and well over 150 events, I have many stories to tell, but I will tell you one from the 9/11 Tribute that George Clooney put together. I was in charge of talent check-in, and Brad Pitt and George were part of our crew. They really did help work on this show. George was helping with the organization of the talent, and Brad was helping with the phone bank. I was assigned to go help Brad once I checked in all the talent. So I went and helped him in that room. After the first round of the talent answering the phone, they all went to the stage and sang and spoke. When everyone exited the stage, Brad and I stood and asked them to come back in and answer the phones for the other coast. Most said no, they were going home. Brad looked at me and said, "I guess no one wants to answer the phones, so do you want to go to dinner?" Airhead me did a complete 360 thinking he was asking someone else. I did not want to make a fool of myself and say yes to see he was talking to someone else behind me. Years before, I thought a singer was waving at me to find out his family was sitting right behind me, so that was all I could think of. I made the entire turn, and no one was there. With my heart pounding, I said, "Sure." He said, "Let's go to the green room and see if there are appetizers left. If not, we will go somewhere else." I was hoping somewhere else, but we got in the elevator, and here was Kelsey Grammar and Robin Williams. We got upstairs, and there were appetizers there. All my years on award shows, I would have normally not stayed with the talent, but this show was so different. After we ate some appetizers, Kelsey and Robin left, Brad and I went back to the talent office, and Julia Roberts and George Clooney were in there with about ten other crew members. We hung out there for a while. It was such a wonderful experience, I still have my credential and a candle from the show, but this was before cameras were on cell phones. Plus, working the award shows, the rule is always you are not a fan. I never took pictures with talent at a show. My career was too important. I have a couple of pictures from after-parties, but very few. I valued the job and experiences way more than risking it for a photo. Plus, I want to be known as a professional when I am working, not a fan. Here are some of my favorite award show pictures.

CHAPTER 10

FROM BAD TO WORSE

My husband was an absolutely fantastic father to my daughter, but he kept getting meaner and meaner to me. He would constantly cut me down in front of my daughter, my family, and our friends. He started drinking more and more. At this point, I believe he was drinking about ten beers a day. I would punish my daughter, and he would come behind me and tell her, "Don't listen to your mom; she's crazy." He did not meet his grandparents until he was sixteen because his mother had gotten in a fight with them and took off to California. So I know in the back of his mind he was worried about abandonment. He always made sure he was the nicer parent and would not back me up on discipline. When she was in elementary school, we even had a group of friends try to talk to him, explaining we needed to parent together and back each other up. He just ignored their advice.

We went on a no-carb diet and switched from beer to vodka. At one point, he got mad at me for something and hit me across the face. I almost left him, but my self-esteem was so low. Luckily, it was already planned for me to go up North the next day to go camping with my parents and visit my high school friends. My daughter and I went and stayed with my parents, and my best friend from high school and her husband supported me through my decision to stay with him. At the time, I did not have the self-esteem or confidence to believe I could afford to raise my daughter on my own. In hindsight, I wish I had the courage to leave then. If I had the finances, I would have done it. It was probably better though that we got her through college together because a custody battle with him would have been a nightmare. I have learned the reason we have to struggle is so we appreciate the growth we achieve and the journey that got us there.

However, the incident did wake my husband up in the sense that he switched back to beer and did not hit me again until my daughter was in college. He did apologize, but after that day, I never felt the same about him. I started cheating on him just to find a way out, praying someone would like me enough to sweep me off my feet and get me out of that situation. I started selling Yellow Page ads to try to make more money, and it was hard for me to balance life. I worked for two different companies; I worked hard and put in so many hours and was successful. I was number one in new accounts at Yellowbook and won Rookie of the year at Verizon. I did settle chasing after smaller accounts because I knew many others were going after the big fish. So my sales were not as high as those of others, but I had consistency. I still worked on the award shows part-time while I was selling Yellowpages.

Life went on, and we bought a toy hauler, mostly for NASCAR races. We loved going infield as a family and with our friends. My daughter became a high school cheerleader, and it became her passion. I went to all the games and competitions. She also did some acting, mostly background, but she had parts in the *Bernie Mac Show*, *Christmas with the Kranks*, and *Cat in the Hat*, to name a few. My parents would bring their motorhome, and we would drive a group of kids to her school dances. Life was pretty normal, but I was honestly miserable and just kept trying to find things to make me happy or make me look and feel popular because I felt so insecure. My work was very high pressure for sales, and I was only popular there when I was selling; any slump, and you were not appreciated.

As far as Nascar, I got involved with the Nascar Members Club and ended up being a chapter leader. I went to a couple of conventions during the All-Star Race, got to meet and have dinner with some of the drivers, and had some amazing experiences. They had me speak at a National Convention about recruiting because I was able to bring members in, and a group of us in Southern California were chosen to Unite our Chapters. I was chosen for an article in the Nascar Members Club Magazine. I enjoyed being part of the club for a few years, but when I got divorced, I just wanted to stay away from my ex-husband, so I chose to stay away from Nascar events because I knew how drunk he got at events and did not want to put myself in that situation. I did have some very fun times for many years at different tracks.

When my daughter turned sixteen, I put so much into giving her a nice sixteenth birthday party. Money was tight, but I purchased all the decorations, plates, etc. Unfortunately, my car ended up breaking down that day.

Both of my moms had it all planned with my daughter to bring different decorations and food. When my car broke down, they would not even come pick me up and take me to the banquet hall. I had to call a friend to come get me when they were at the hall a mile away. By the time I got there, they said, "We don't need your stuff. We're doing it this way." To them, it was no big deal, but it crushed me. I had put so much time and planning into trying to give my daughter the best party. The party turned out very nice, but the disrespect of all my time and planning was just another time that my family made me feel so unimportant. They have no clue all these little incidents created more low self-esteem. I feel my daughter has no respect for me because of the way her dad and my family treated me all through her high school years, and to this day, she still does not. I've tried everything to show her love, but my words constantly get misconstrued. She blames me for things her dad told her that never even happened. One night, I punished her, and her dad walked

up and said, "Don't listen to your mom; she's just a bitch."
Then she would say to me, "Mom, I'm not listening to you.
All I have to do is bat my eyes at Dad, and he will let me
do it anyway." We were so close when she was little, and I
did everything for her. One night, she told me that she
only remembers hanging out with Dad, that I never did
things with her. I did everything in my power to show her
love and still try to. She's maturing but is still angry with
me. I know I am far from perfect, but I am a good honest
person with a very kind heart. I get blamed for so much
that other people would not be blamed for. Sometimes,
because I am not quick and witty, the right words do not
come out, and I look back and say, "I wish I would have
said this. Or why didn't I think of this at the time." It has
taken me a long time to learn you can not please everyone,
and if they do not value that I am a good honest person, I
can not change them. I will never give up on my daughter
or my parents, but there are enough other people in the

world. If they do not respect me, I have learned to move on and find other people who give me respect.

CHAPTER 11

LIVE LIKE YOU ARE DYING

In 2008 and 2009, I kept having asthma attacks. I was working out of Palm Springs and staying at a condo there that Verizon (Super Media), who I worked for at the time, paid for. They were reseeding, and I kept having breathing issues. It was embarrassing when I could barely walk upstairs, and I had trouble giving sales presentations. I had sixteen asthma attacks in three months. I was able to control many of them, but in February, I had to go to the hospital the day after being at the speedway for a NASCAR race. What is so strange is that day was the one and only time nurses were at my office doing physicals, and I passed the physical in the morning, but that afternoon, all of a sudden, another asthma attack came on. This asthma attack was really, really bad. I left work early because I couldn't breathe. I just kept gasping for air, and about two hours after I got home, I was breathing so bad I woke up my husband, and I could barely get the words out to tell him I needed to get to the emergency room. The song "Live Like You Are Dying" came on as we were driving, and I honestly believed I *was* dying. The only way I can describe an asthma attack is like drowning; you're gasping for air so bad you can barely feel it.

My husband took me to the closest urgent care. In hindsight, I wish we would have gone to the local hospital, as things might have gone differently. When we arrived, I was in such bad shape. The nurse forgot to take my vitals. They just rushed me in and straight to the machines. They had me breathe into the nebulizer, but it was not enough.

I was sitting on the bed trying to breathe into the machine and take in the medicine, and I passed out, for just a few seconds, I think. But the next thing I knew, they were giving me a shot. I lost control of my bodily functions and was shaking and squirming like a fish. They kept me there until they closed. I was so exhausted and worn out I think I slept for a couple of days after I got home. When I woke up, I had a terrible brain fog, and it still has not left all these years later. My speech, memory, coordination, processing have all been different since that night.

The first neurologist I went to told me I was just depressed. Then I went to the pain medicine doctor I had been going to for my fibromyalgia, and he noticed I was slurring words. I explained what had happened, and he sent me to a different neurologist. That neurologist found deterioration in my brain. In fact, part of my brain was not there, a.k.a. the True Airhead. He sent me to UCLA, where I underwent eight hours of testing. They had to wake me up twice during the testing because I got so exhausted I would fall asleep. I had to call my daughter and my dad to come get me because there was no way I could physically drive home. Two weeks later, we went back for the results. They gave me recommendations for physical therapy and a neuropsychologist and told me to put something social on my calendar every day. They did not care what I did as long as I did something daily. The doctor said, "I have seen too many patients with successful careers go into major depression because all of a sudden they have all this extra time and don't know what to do with it, so they go into a depression."

Honestly, until COVID, I stuck with the doctor's philosophy and spent way too much money socializing through the years. I tried going back to school. I took a math class, but it took me four to five hours to do the homework. I had to face that I was not capable. I spent a lot of time in the disability lab, but with my short-term memory and processing issues, I could not concentrate enough. I had speech therapy, and they called me in very stumped; they said, "We have never seen this before. Your spelling, math, and grammar are at this certain percent, but your mapping is perfect." I explained, "I worked for the Yellowpages for years and charted my route and territory every day." So, somehow, that stayed with me. Overall I still have a very good sense of direction.

For three years, I also tried to improve my breathing. They tried so many different procedures and treatments, like taking out my uvula, giving me very heavy steroids, etc., to try to help me control my breathing. I even got a breast reduction to see if taking weight off would make a difference, which it did not.

Around that time, I also ended up needing a hysterectomy. My family always rushed to the hospital when someone was sick. When I was in the hospital, however, my mom and all my siblings on her side of the family all went on vacation and drove right by the hospital. My parents and brother drove within ten minutes of the hospital on their way to Big Bear. That crushed my self-esteem so badly. To me, it was like, why is everyone in my family always there for anyone else but me? They drive right past the hospital on their way to vacation and cannot even stop and say hi or text me that they are thinking of me? My youngest brother is the only one I got a message from the day of the surgery. I was already in such a desperate place with being cut down all the time by my husband and the adjustments from the brain damage. From that day on, I just felt so unloved and unwanted by my family. It bothered me so bad that they all could drive by the hospital, spend all weekend parting together, but not even stop for ten minutes by a hospital they were passing two hours from their house. Or stop by my house on their way home when I had just gotten out of the hospital. Emotions came out every time I tried to speak to them, and I constantly cried around them. I have been told that the tears come from the scars that were planted deep within me. I try to control them, but with my family, the hurt is so deep I cannot stop crying, especially when they cut me down—I can go on for hours with stories of hurt and disrespect towards me. Don't get me wrong; my family are all good people. They just honestly do not know how to deal with emotional situations. They think it's better to avoid things and let them pass. For some reason, to me, they are like bullies. They all stick together but think it is okay to exclude me and make me feel completely unwanted because I am emotional. Yet, they can not see their treatment towards me created the emotions, and they will not apologize. Unfortunately, just like with the word "love," the word "sorry" will not come out. There is no empathy when it comes to me. I just do not know how to get them to understand every tear comes from scares and is out of love trying to fit into their mold. No child should ever have to beg their parents to love them. I understand tough love for drugs but for someone who does not take drugs, no matter how old you are, when you see photos of your family getting together or going on vacations, and you are not invited, it is beyond hurtful.

For example, my dad got angry with me when I showed him my brain damage report. Instead of saying, "I love you. I'll be there for you," he said, "This report is wrong. I don't believe it." A family friend that was there who lost her dad totally started defending my dad. I was lost and devastated my spelling, grammar, math, and coordination have changed, and here, instead of support and hugs, I am being told the doctors are wrong; they don't believe the MRI showing a piece of my brain missing. My neuropsychologist tried having a meeting with my parents, and my dad brought a list of texts and things he felt I did wrong. We tried to have a discussion and got nowhere. This doctor was the third doctor to tell me just to stay away from my family because, unfortunately, they had no empathy. "No matter how hard you try," he said, "they will never see your side. They will never be supportive of you." I will never understand how someone can murder someone and have their family be in a courthouse and completely support them and show them love, but yet, here I get a brain injury, and my family treats me like I am this horrible person, stops inviting me to events, and blames me for being overdramatic. All I wanted was love from them. I was so scared and adapting to the life changes, I needed a support system to boost my confidence, not be told it is not true and don't listen to the doctors.

I still try to stay in contact with my family, but there's such a distance. Right before I got divorced, we went on a trip with my mom and the brothers and sisters on her side to the wineries. My asthma started acting up, and I had an inhaler in my purse, but somehow I lost it at one of the wineries. I was so out of breath I needed to go get a new inhaler from the hotel. They had me call an Uber, and they all stayed, going from winery to winery. Not one family member would go with me even though I couldn't even breathe. I was gasping for air on the Uber ride and when walking to the hotel room. It was so bad I almost called 911. My own husband would not even go when I was so out of breath. In their eyes, I was being dramatic. That just made me more desperate to get out of the marriage. Years later, I found out wine spilled on a bedspread at the hotel, and they charged my sister. My mom paid for it but didn't tell me about it, but they had judgment and anger over something I never even knew happened. I mentioned this before, but it truly bothers me so bad when people are not upfront and don't communicate but talk behind people's backs to others. Next time a situation comes up, think, "Should I gossip about it or go straight to that person and truly deal with the situation?" Things will never improve or change if the person your gossiping about does not know you are feeling that way. There is also a nice way to approach things, but with my family, I have made some mistakes because I have been so hurt and I got extremely emotional. It is the years

of cut downs and being made fun of crying out. I can not
control the crying no matter how hard I try.

CHAPTER 12

HAD TO FIND
MY WAY OUT!

The next three years were a blur of surgeries and trying to live life. I was going to physical, vision, and speech therapy, and my daughter was going to college. A popular local brewery became my hangout, and I made a big group of friends that became a great support system for me. I felt so much better when I was outdoors than in that house. My parents would get frustrated with me, thinking, "Why are you drinking if you are so sick?" For me, it was not even about the drinking; it was going there for the social interaction. I had so many friends there and loved the outdoors. I didn't realize then, but I was so desperate to find a way out of my relationship and that house I would have done almost anything to get out of that situation. I absolutely loved hanging out there, making friends, and getting attention at a place where I was spoken to with respect. My life was so much better when I was there, and people talked to me, and I could breathe better than when I was at home being out of breath, cut down, and screamed at by my future ex-husband at this point.

The day after one of my surgeries, my husband got in a car accident on his way to work. He called his best friend from the hospital and did not even let me know he was in the hospital. He said it was because I was recovering from my surgery. That really hurt my feelings. In my eyes, what kind of relationship am I in when your husband is in the hospital and calls the best friend instead of you? He was not even that close with his best friend. In fact, if you asked that best friend who his best friend was, I guarantee you it would not be him. I was already so uncomfortable in our marriage, and that was just another checkmark for me as to our relationship was ending. I was so hurt over him not calling me and letting me know he was in a car accident but calling the friend to pick him up. I know I was down from surgery, but have the courtesy to let me know what is happening. He knew I was already so hurt that my family didn't come visit me in the hospital, and now he was in the hospital and did not let me know he was there. It just made me feel so unloved. It made me more determined to get out of the situation.

My husband was drinking so much at home he would never go out with me. I was practically living a single life, just desperately trying to find a way out. I was working an event for the TV show *Biggest Loser*, so I talked my husband into going with me, and we got a room at the Queen Mary. He was so rude to me at the restaurant, and when he got up to go to the restroom, the waitress came to me and said, "You seem like such a sweet lady. You deserve better. He is horrible to you. Please try to build some confidence to get out." That just got me more desperate trying to find a way out. I look back now and wish I would have just rented a room from someone, but at the time, I honestly did not feel I could afford to.

Then, on the 4th of July, I talked him into going to a concert at the park with a group of friends. He was talking so rudely to me that a girl that never even met him took some duct tape and stuck it on his mouth. She told him, "How dare you talk to your wife like that!" Later that evening, we went to a friend's house to watch the fireworks. I went to the restroom, and he came in behind me. As I was sitting on the toilet, he grabbed my arms roughly and said, "I'm going first," and threw me out of the restroom with my pants still partially down. The next day, I had bruises up my arms. I went home that night, slept on the couch, and tried to figure out how I was going to leave. God answered. My mom called and said my Nana was sick and asked if I could come to take care of her. I stayed with her for a month. I did, and it was so hard, I was with her 24/7. Every time a family member came, I would go for a hike. She had a park by her house with all these trails that used to be a movie set. I loved escaping and just hiking around that park and on all of the trials.

Then I agreed to go to Montana for a family reunion. At this point, I was so uncomfortable around him, but I tried to rescue my marriage for our twenty-fifth anniversary. He was so horrible to me there, my parents pulled me aside and said, "You have to get out. We don't care if you live in our motorhome, but he's just horrible to you." After being married for twenty-five years, I was scared, but I knew I needed to go.

On our way home, one good thing was we stopped by Bear World in Rexburg, Idaho, and went to Yellowstone for a day. So at least I got some nature and beauty in to try to change the pace. Then, driving home, I was texting a male friend. At this point, I was so desperate I was just trying to find a knight in shining armor to rescue me. I didn't think I could afford things on my own, and I lived near my doctors and friends. I wasn't sure I could move into my parents' motorhome, as they lived a couple of hours away. My husband yelled at me the whole way back to where we were staying, at a cousin's house in Salt Lake, twenty-five minutes away. When I took over driving, he said, "You're not texting or talking on your phone." As I was driving, the phone rang. He said, "I'll answer it." I said, "No, you said I can't text or talk. We're twenty minutes away. I'll deal with it then." Well, his mom had had a stroke and refused to take the stroke medicine. She refused the medicine because there was a chance of death from the medicine. When we got to my cousin's, I returned the call, and it was the hospital. We got a hold of the doctor, and he said the medicine would not have worked anyway with the type of stroke she had. But we were too late; she hit the two-hour mark for the medicine. My husband thought he could have talked her into taking the medicine, so in his eyes, it was my fault for not picking up the phone. So you can imagine he was even madder at me than he already was. To this day, he blames me for his mom not getting the stroke medicine even though the doctors made it very clear it would not have worked with the kind of stroke she had. Her stroke caused her to be completely paralyzed on her left side, and all of her food has to be pureed because she can no longer chew properly. As soon as I got home, I went straight back to taking care of my Nana. There were too many issues with his mom, so I was forced to go back home.

Once home, I reached my last straw. I had to deal with his mom and get her into an assisted living situation. One day, I had gone to the hospital to see her in the morning, fit in two doctor's appointments, met with her doctors, and looked at three facilities for my mother-in-law to move into. I walked into her hospital room, and there was food all over her face. She had to have her food puréed because of the stroke because she couldn't swallow. I walked into the room, and there was food all over her. My mother-in-law told me my daughter fed her. I knew that was the day before because she had not been there that day. I asked the nurse why she had left her the food instead of helping her eat, and she apologized and said she forgot. I called my husband and daughter and asked if one of them could please come for her dinner and make sure everything was okay because I had bunco at six. They said, "No, we're at home drinking and having fun." I had to get a sub for bunco, stayed for her dinner, and said, "I'm done. I'm getting a hotel tonight. I can't do this anymore." They begged me to come home, and I said, "Well, get my prescription," because the pharmacy was closing before I could get there. I pulled into where the pharmacy was, and my daughter just started yelling at me. I was so worn out and exhausted, and the disrespect I got from her was just too much for me to handle physically and mentally. I gave my husband the wedding ring back and said, "I do not deserve this disrespect. I'm done." My daughter begged me to stay until her twenty-first birthday because she was so afraid people would not come to her party if her father and I were separated. From that point on, I did everything I could to stay away from that house and figure out a way out. I went back to my Nana's again but kept getting calls to take care of stuff for my mother-in-law, who was two hours away. I ended up back at home with my husband until my daughter's birthday in November and went on dates trying to find someone to rescue me. I was so desperate to find a way out. My self-esteem was so low. I just wanted someone who would love and respect me. I look back now and have no idea why I didn't think I could afford to rent a room from someone. I wish I would have had the confidence to leave in July and not have stuck it out until her birthday. In my mind, I left on July 4th after he pushed me out of the bathroom. That is the day I was done as far as I felt. A lot of people may disagree with me, but in my eyes, I felt I was not cheating after that day. As far as I was concerned, I was separated, and my marriage was done. The love had been gone for so long; incident after incident was just another checkmark. If I had the money I would have left way before with no issues. I did that 100 percent for her, but she still brings it up and is bitter that I left on her birthday. There was no winning in that situation. I stayed for her but am still the horrible person for leaving, even though she knew her dad was an alcoholic and very mean to me.

A very successful businessman that was in an organization I belonged to asked me if I could come to take care of him because he was having back surgery. There was my answer. He was sixteen years older and had not lived with anyone for thirty years. There were so many bad warning signs, but I was so desperate I saw none of them. He wasn't charging me rent, so I could pay off bills. I needed out of the other situation so badly I didn't even see what I was doing to myself or my reputation. He was so nice and good to me when I first moved in. He had two houses, one at a beautiful gated community with activities. I was swept off my feet and so happy. My daughter was so angry at me. How dare I leave! Things went great until he had his back surgery. Once he recovered from the surgery, he did a complete 180. I learned what a huge narcissist he was. He said things like, "We both used each other." My insecurity went way worse because now I had this situation I was living in where I was being treated horribly again.

I was scheduled for surgery to put steroids into my lungs because my vocal cords were still closing up, and I still had issues with my asthma. I went to the pre-op, and the doctor said, "What did you do differently?" I said, "I separated from my husband and moved out of my house." He said, "For the first time in five years, your lungs are clear. We are going to cancel the surgery, and you don't need another appointment." I asked the doctor, "Could it have been mold? There was a sprinkler that sprayed on our old house. I hired two gardeners to fix it, and my ex turned them away, saying he would do it." My arms would get so large on mold when I took an allergy test, so that must have been the issue. I have not had an asthma attack since I moved out of that house in 2012. I have not had a major one since 2009, but that was because they had me on such high doses of steroids and other medicines since 2009. Once I moved out in 2012, I have not had the shortness of breath I used to get. I borrowed money from my parents to put a down payment on an apartment. Some friends helped me get nine pieces of furniture from my old house. After twenty-five years of marriage, that's all I got. My ex-husband stood and controlled everything that was packed up. He grabbed the screws to my bed. Supposedly, he could not find them. Two days later, I went back to get the screws, and he handed them to me and then grabbed my wrist so tightly I had a huge bruise that lasted over a week. He said, "I just wanted to screw with you." After that, I made sure I was never alone with him. Another time, I went to visit his mother, and he grabbed me in the parking lot and bruised my arms again, so, unfortunately, I stopped going to visit his mom. He was a reserve police officer out of the station where we lived, and so I was not comfortable turning him in. Plus, I know if I turned him in, my daughter would never forgive me.

That just put me in a more desperate spot, two breakups from men that just did not respect me. I swore I would never let anyone disrespect me again. This may have caused some of my family tension, but after that, I was not going to let anyone cut me down or disrespect me. I know I deserve respect, and if you don't feel the same, I don't want to be around you. All I wanted out of life was to be loved by someone.

I went into such a desperate, lonely place. I hated living alone. I dated everyone I could until I met an amazing man, Randy. He is a very hard-working businessman who works for a large corporation. On our first date, he talked about going to Hawaii in two months. We just clicked personality-wise; he was different than I was, but I could tell he was an honest, genuine person who truly cared. We either saw each other or talked on the phone every day for those two months. I was so nervous about going to Hawaii with someone I hardly knew but was excited at the same time. We went to Hawaii and had a fabulous time. We spent a lot of time swimming with turtles, took a helicopter ride, went to a Hawaiian Luau, took a flight from Maui to Oahu for a day, went to Pearl Harbor, and by coincidence, my youngest brother and parents were there, so we meet them for dinner before we flew back to Maui. The trip was so incredible; he swept me off my feet for sure. On the flight home, Randy started having trouble breathing. After we got home that afternoon, we went to the local brewery, and he had a beer, and his breathing got worse. We ended up having to take him to the emergency room. The look on his face when

Randy asked me to "please stay with him and not leave him alone" will be etched in my memory forever. He ended up in the hospital for three days with very bad pneumonia. After that, he would start to get better and then get sick again.

We went to my mom's house, and Randy said to me, "You are the kindest, sweetest person I've ever met. Why does your family treat you like a black sheep?" That was the fourth person in my life to ask me why my family treated me differently. The feeling of being rejected and not wanted by your own family makes it very hard to feel secure and confident. I literally begged for their love, but in their eyes, I am just a negative, complaining victim. No matter how hard I begged for them to see what I was feeling, they would just push me further away. Years before, a family friend said, "Why does your dad favor your sister and act like you don't exist?" That made me feel so insecure and awkward. How are you supposed to answer a question like that?

116

I was still living in the apartment, waiting on my divorce. Money was really tight for me, and my ex-husband would not let me have access to my stuff. They need to change the laws. He was sitting pretty in the house with everything we owned and had changed the locks, so I had access to nothing. You don't think about all the basics, like pens, tape, scissors, silverware, dishes, etc., until you don't have them and have to buy them. I only had $125 in my bank account, and because of the law, I would have to go to court and hire an attorney before I could get anything from my ex. I remember I was so bad off that one day, Randy and I went to a store, and he gave a man sitting outside a $20 bill. I said to him, "I can't believe you gave him that much money!" To him, $20 was nothing. To me, it was lunch for a week. Two years later, I finally got my clothes because the judge ordered him to give them to me. By that time, I had purchased a new wardrobe—I had to. When I went to get the clothes, the walkway where the broken sprinkler was was lifted up like it had exploded and was all muddy. All the leaking water had created a mud pile where rock steps used to be. My ex hid so many of my outfits. I had a friend who was am ex-professional football player go with me. My ex-husband had hoarded the house so bad he had to lift me to grab the clothes. I think he purposely put stuff in front of closets just so it was harder to get to. When I finally got them, all my business suits either had just the jacket or just the pants or skirts. I had a signed football jersey that he said got lost, etc. Not to mention the rest of my family did a complete 180 on me. Even though they told me to get out, they were completely on my ex's side.

My Nana passed away, and Randy and I went to the funeral. My mom wanted my ex to sing at the funeral. I told them I was not comfortable with that. I personally was not comfortable with him being at the funeral, let alone singing and being up there. My family could not understand why I did not want this man who was violent towards me up there singing at the funeral of someone so special to me. I lost; they let him sing. Again, it made me sick to my stomach. Then my mom invited him in the family party bus on the way to the cemetery that was just for immediate family. Randy and I were so uncomfortable. My daughter was sitting next to me, and my mom was hanging out with him like he was his best friend. We stopped and went to the restroom, and everyone went back to their same seat, but my mom and ex-husband took our seats and just laughed as we got back on. Maybe I take things the wrong way sometimes, but that really bothered me. I am so uncomfortable being in the same room with him because I do not know if he is going to grab my wrist again. He is such an alcoholic; who knows if he will just hit Randy one day. Randy is not the violent type, but he is on a lot of medicines and does not drink much, so he is what is considered a lightweight when it comes to alcohol. I just do not want to be in a situation where something could happen. It is okay for my family to avoid me and cut me out of events, but they feel that because he is my daughter's father, he should be invited even though he was violent towards me. All I have wanted is my family's understanding as to why I was scared to be around him. Again the lack of understanding as to why I did not want him around just brought my self-confidence and self-esteem to an even lower point.

The following Christmas, my parents wanted me to spend Christmas with this man who was horrible to me. He would get so drunk, and I did not want to be in that situation. After he bruised my arms twice, I was honestly scared and uncomfortable to be around him. I tried to explain that to them, but it did not matter; they still invited him. I get the years mixed up. There was one year we went but left instead of staying the night like we always did; another year, we did not go, and another year, they just invited us finally.

CHAPTER 13

RANDY AND

I FOUND PARADISE

Randy and I bought an amazing house in Canyon Lake, California. They call Canyon Lake "a little piece of paradise," and it truly is. We had been looking at smaller houses with boat docks, and then the realtor said, "Let me show you this house. It does not have a boat dock, but it has a beautiful view, and you can get double the house for the same money." Randy did not want to go. His attitude was, "If it doesn't have a boat dock, I don't want to see it." I finally talked him into just looking at it. It had a big, beautiful kitchen. The realtor was talking to Randy when I went upstairs to a huge open room with a bar and an amazing view of the lake. I said, "Randy, come look up here." He walked up, looked at our bar, and said, "Can't you just see our Redlands friends hanging out here?" Then he turned around, and his mouth dropped. There was stained glass with hot air balloons, and he said, "I've seen those balloons in a dream. I'm done. This is it." It was more than I wanted to spend, but there was no talking to him about any other house. This was it. I joke I feel like Cinderella sometimes in this beautiful home. It is hard for me to keep up, and Randy works so much it is all on my shoulders. But I feel so blessed living here. Waking up to the water view is like being on vacation every day. We had to borrow money from my parents and his sister until I got my divorce settlement. Here is our beautiful house and view from the patio. We love living near the water.

We embraced Canyon Lake. They had so many activities and clubs for many different things. The clubs were closed for the summer, and friends that I thought would come visit did not. I almost went into a depression as I was unpacking and getting the house ready. Then I started water aerobics, and we joined many clubs, and I just flourished. We have had many fundraisers at our house. I love entertaining and people enjoying our home. For the first time in my life, I really felt respected (besides some friends who have always respected me). Many people have told me how popular we are here. We have made so many great friends within this community.

Randy kept getting pneumonia, and each time, his breathing got a little worse. We decided to get married, mostly for medical reasons. He got put in ICU, and they would not let me in until visiting hours because I was not immediate family. Here we owned a house together, but that did not matter. I love him so much, but I did question marrying him because he was sick. Randy was getting to where he did not like to do certain things because he was so tired and so short of breath. But I knew this man loved me, and he puts up with all the mistakes I make due to my brain damage—even though he gets frustrated with me because I cannot keep the house up sometimes.

Our wedding was absolutely beautiful. We got married on May 2, 2015, at the beach eight houses down, right in front of the lake. There was a lot of family drama, but I'm not even going to go through all that. We had a beautiful wedding with fantastic friends and family, a great day overall. It was Randy's idea for me to arrive at the beach in a golf cart to the song Tammy. Then as I walked down the aisle, he sang, "You are so beautiful to me." Most of my family was there, but unfortunately, I didn't feel the love and support I had at my first wedding. I am still thankful they were all there, though. They have no idea what it's like to live completely exhausted all the time and not be able to concentrate and stay organized. They look at me and think, "You look normal. You're just trying to play the victim." I wish they could live in my body for twenty minutes to see what I feel on a daily basis, to see how hard it is to focus and concentrate, especially if I'm tired. We had a lot of wonderful friends at the wedding too, and it went absolutely wonderful.

As time went on, Randy started getting sicker and sicker. His breathing turned into wheezing and gasping for air. He wore oxygen anytime he walked somewhere more than a few feet. He had this big cord so he could walk through the house. Sometimes, he would trip over it. It was hard for him to do a simple task at this point; I think he was still working but tired.

On my fiftieth birthday, we went to Vegas and the Garth Brooks concert. We hung out with friends and family. Randy was so bad off he needed a wheelchair to get around. Everyone stayed at the same hotel except for my mom and daughter. I kept having to leave my friends at the pool to go let them in. In a Vegas casino hotel, that's like a twenty-minute walk each way. The night of my birthday, my mom and daughter decided they didn't want to go to the restaurant I had picked out. Then my mom started inviting my friends and family to another restaurant instead. That was my day, and it was hard enough getting Randy to the venue with a scooter. I do not understand why my family is so inconsiderate of my feelings and my plans. My mom apologized after we got home, but my daughter did not and was very upset that I wouldn't go to the other restaurant. It was over a mile walk from the venue. She came all the way to Vegas for my fiftieth birthday and did not spend more than a couple of hours with me. They tried to ruin my plans, which put other people in an awkward situation, and in my mom's and daughter's eyes, it was all my fault. My family would never do that to another family member, but they guilt-tripped me for not wanting to change my plans even though it was my birthday. They had no respect for me. Not to mention the fact that Randy was having so much trouble breathing and getting around he did not want to go that extra mile. The whole day turned into a big fiasco.

Randy kept getting pneumonia. Then, one day, we went to his pulmonologist, who said, "Randy needs a double lung transplant." We were like, "What? A transplant?" We didn't know anything about transplants, and we were very scared. We were just shaking, but my friend had told me about a very funny movie the week before. So on our way home from the doctor, I told Randy, let's just get our mind off things and go see a funny movie. Well, the movie was *Florence Foster Jenkins* with Meryl Streep. It was not a comedy, it was a drama-romance, and in the end, there's a death. It was the worst movie I could have taken him to. Airhead me trusted what my friend said instead of researching the movie. We were shaking so badly and scared, and this movie did not help.

CHAPTER 14

THE CARETAKER: RANDY'S DOUBLE LUNG TRANSPLANT

Randy was so nervous about the transplant. A coworker of his passed away on the operating table, and another coworker had a heart attack in the car as he was driving them to the hospital. So the thought of a transplant really terrified Randy. He was so afraid that he would not live through it. I mentioned to a friend at a fundraiser at our house that we were scared and

Randy was not sure if he wanted the transplant, especially since we had been told by the doctor and read on the internet that they only lasted six years. They told us about someone from our neighborhood who had a double lung transplant and was going on for over twenty years. We said, "No, it can't be. They only last six years." We set up to go to dinner with the neighbor who had the lung transplant, and Randy did a complete 180. He was then ready and excited to get on the transplant list. Very scared and anxious, but ready for a new lease on life. Ready for the ultimate gift of life from a donor. In the middle of all this, he became paranoid that our house needed to be ready to sell in case he died. However, he was afraid the house would not sell if the kitchen was not repainted, so he insisted we get that done before the transplant. Money was so tight for us at that point, I begged him not to, but there was no reasoning with him. It was all just anxiety.

We could not go more than two hours from our house while Randy was on the transplant list. We missed

Christmas with my family, and a group of our close friends went on a cruise for New Year's. We went and worked on a Rose Parade Float that night instead. By this point, Randy was on oxygen twenty-four hours a day and needed a walker or wheelchair if we were walking more than a few feet. While working on the Rose Parade Float, we had a lady tell us, "Please do not be scared if you're offered a high-risk donor. Times are different today, and they do so much testing." Every time the phone would ring, our heart would skip a beat, hoping that was the call.

I worked the Grammys on February 12 and then the tribute to the Bee Gees on February 14. I ended up with a sore throat, so Randy told me to stay in LA for the 15th and rest. Randy had a doctor's appointment on the morning of the 17th, and since I wasn't feeling well, the night of the 16th when I got home, we decided to get a hotel in San Diego because Randy had to be at labs at 7:30 a.m. before his appointment. At 6:30 a.m. on February 17, we got a call saying they had a lung for him. But it was high risk because the donor had used drugs with an IV. Randy said yes right away, and they told him to cancel his doctor's appointment and wait for the phone call. The call woke us up, so our hearts did not stop the way it did other rings, but this was the call we were waiting for. When we got the call, we were nervous but so ready. My parents drove to San Diego and were there at the hospital. The day they had to fly the lungs in, we were in a room at the hospital from 1 p.m. until about 11 p.m. They took him in about 11 p.m. on the 17th. They operated for nine hours that night. Because my throat was a little scratchy, the hospital staff did not want me there on the first day. But my parents were there for him, and at that point, people could only see him through the glass anyway. By the next day, my throat was fine, and Randy's sister flew in and spent a week. I was there outside the glass when his sister arrived. I went downstairs to get her and bring her up, and within ten minutes, they had taken the ventilator out. We walked up and took a picture of him smiling through the glass with a big thumbs-up. He has not needed oxygen since that day.

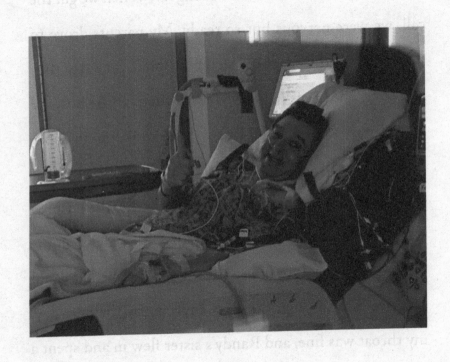

Randy leaving a rose in memory of his donor.

He got out of the hospital a week later, and we stayed at a hotel, as they required we stay close by. I made a big airhead mistake. I bought soups and vegetables for a hot plate we had in our room. I bought low-sodium soup, thinking I was being healthy, and his potassium levels went too high. I had no idea that these foods had lots of potassium and would be bad for him. They had to change his medicines because of the high potassium. He progressed amazingly through his transplant. Words can not express how thankful we are for the gift of life from his donor. We have written to the donor family but have been told they are not interested in contact with us. I pray one day they can meet Randy and see what the gift of life has done to change our life and made it so Randy is able to live a productive life. If you are not a registered donor, please see how it has saved my husband's life and consider becoming one.

We stayed away from people for a month after the surgery, and he wore a mask and gloves everywhere he went—that was way before COVID. After a month, we went to brunch with a group of our closest friends. They were so supportive, and we all just hugged and cried when we saw each other. Money was so tight because of the hotel and house payments, so some friends helped us raise some money. Unfortunately, we had a small group of neighbors who didn't think we deserved help because we had painted our kitchen cupboards. They will never understand the anxiety Randy had before the transplant. I do not know why I get judged so much more than most people do. Some people just don't accept me the way they accept others. We lost some friends over the rumors. Again, I didn't have the confidence to realize it their problem: they were too weak to stand up to the bullies that started the rumors. It hurt my self-esteem to lose some friends, but we realized we don't want to be around people that talk behind our backs. We stuck with our true friends and are still very close to them. They are like family to us. They have been our support system, especially for laughs and giggles. I am not the best at staying in contact with people, but just know, if you are my friend and you are reading this book, I appreciate you more than I can ever express.

A year later, Randy went back to work. He was a nervous wreck and had so much anxiety about going back. We went on vacation, and he was just miserable. I did not know it at the time, but now I have learned how to deal with him when he gets anxious. My neuropsychologist really helped me figure that out. Once I did, Randy and I have had a great relationship.

It has not been 100 percent roses, though. Randy has had cancer ten times since the transplant. He has had different kinds of cancer—in his stomach, esophagus, both ears, nose, neck, and a few on his back and face. He is having a process called photopheresis, which is a

$500,000 procedure—thank goodness for insurance—where they are removing his blood via a machine, cleaning it through a photo process, and then returning it. This procedure is so he will not have to take one of the anti-rejection drugs he needs to take daily that they think could be causing the cancers. Other than that, he has been completely healthy and has been a complete workaholic since he went back to work.

CHAPTER 15

YEP: THE BREAKTHROUGH FREEDOM CHALLENGE THAT CHANGED MY LIFE

When COVID hit, one of my coworkers from the award shows passed away. He was healthy just a couple of weeks before running around at the Grammys. It really shook me when he died. All I could think of is I would feel so guilty if I got Randy sick. Because I worked audience Department my career working award shows stopped instantly thanks to covid. Plus, I was so worried about Randy and his transplant, I decided to find a job at home. Randy's boss moved him into a facility that only had seven employees. They made arrangements, so he really was not near the other employees even though he went into work every day. My best friend and I started selling Color Street nail strips, and it was very successful for us the first few months. Then they hired so many reps it was hard to make a profit. We are still selling them, but it's just a little hobby now. We found an arts and crafts company that was on the ground floor, and we were super excited about it. Then the owner took off with everyone's money, and all the months I spent working on building the business were just a waste of my time. Then I tried another company that I just floundered at. My self-esteem took a huge hit: I was putting so many hours in and getting nowhere financially.

Then I went to a free five-day challenge from an entrepreneurial community. The community was called

YEP, Young Entrepreneur Project. This is a group of entrepreneurs who are so warm and giving. They want to help each other, with the philosophy that we will all be more successful as a team than being lone wolves out there trying to do it by ourselves.

When I found this group, I was just physically and mentally drained. I went into a VIP group in the challenge and was looking down at my phone, trying to invite people to the challenge. I was so inspired by the challenge that I wanted to share it with everyone. The guest speaker, Willy Tubbs, said, "Tammy, I need you to focus." I was listening but looking down, and I jumped up, startled, and he said, "Tammy, turn on your mic, tell me something that's different about you than everyone else on this call." I said, "I am a true airhead. Part of my brain is missing." He said, "Why are you not marketing that?" I said, "Because I do my best not to be made fun of." He said, "That is marketable. You need to write a book, and I will help you do it. I said, "I don't think it's possible. My spelling and grammar are horrible." Dr. Breakthrough, Stan Harris, jumped in and said, "Yes, a breakthrough! I will help you with that too. Don't worry about that part. There are editors for that. We can make it happen." Another author, Lynda Joyce, messaged me and also offered to help. It was almost like a religious experience. There were so many emotions as I cried, but yet I knew it was the right thing. My confidence level instantly changed because of all the emails and support I got from people within that community. For about a month, every time I went to talk, tears would run down my face. That community has honestly changed my life, and I welcome anyone reading this to contact me, and I can arrange for you to go through this life-changing challenge.

A couple of weeks later, Randy and I had to fly to Michigan because his dad was so sick. Obviously, that made me even more emotional and drained at the time. We had a wonderful week with his dad and got to say our goodbyes before he passed in complete peace. Randy got a week's bereavement, and we told very few people because of COVID; we just didn't want judgment. We changed our flight and went to a summit in Florida and meetings with some people from YEP. I got to meet my mentors, Jimmy Ezzell, Gina Easton, and Dr. Breakthrough, as well as some other great members of the community. Randy went to some events and also rested and relaxed. He was emotionally drained after losing his dad. Jennifer Norris spoke and talked about my breakthrough in her speech. She said, "If you don't think you can do it, just go ask Tammy Revard." It made me feel so good to be recognized by a community that appreciates everyone's efforts.

My income has increased with YEP. I've won additional money for recruiting people because I have so much conviction about this community. Both Willy Tubbs and Dr. Breakthrough have invited me to do testimonials at events, and I'm getting much better and stronger each time I speak.

I grew up learning sales skills from Zig Ziglar's books. I had the honor to do a testimonial right after Tom Ziglar, Zig Ziglar's son, spoke. My parents were on that Zoom. I felt that would make a difference to them, seeing I was achieving things; unfortunately, it did not. I have learned you cannot change someone else's mindset, and some people will not align with what you believe in. Just be your true authentic self, have consistency and conviction. If you have the mindset to make the changes and do the work to change, the right people will come to you. No matter if you're in Direct Sales, Network Marketing, an entrepreneur or not: do not worry about what other people think of you and start thinking about what you can do to help others. If you want to succeed, you need to find mentors who are doing what you want to do better. Invest in yourself. It may be scary if money is tight, but if you associate and learn from the right people, take in and implement what they say, and have the confidence within yourself to change your mindset, you can fly to the top.

CHAPTER 16
AFFIRMATIONS

In a Club House room, this man named Bliss heard my story and asked to schedule a Zoom call with me. He told me he wanted to do an affirmation. I honestly had no clue what that was, and the back of my mind was thinking, "What does he want from me?" Bliss just had a very kind heart who wanted to do this affirmation for me. He interviewed me and asked me some questions about what I wanted in life. He put together this affirmation for me.

~ *Tammy* ~

I am a great
COMMUNICATOR.
I am DYNAMIC and
FINANCIALLY FREE.
I am able to HELP OTHERS
and I ATTRACT the
RIGHT PEOPLE to me.
I am thankful to
SHARE MY STORY
and turn my experiences
into something new.
I am thankful for
the ways in which
I can GIVE VALUE.

I have done my best to read it every day. I truly believe I will change my life and achieve everything on this list. After he did this for me, I keep hearing the word "affirmation" from people. A mastermind I am into did a class on Affirmations a few weeks later. I was glued to the computer and loving it, so much so just from those two experiences, I actually was asked to teach a class, and so I did it on writing affirmations, and it went absolutely wonderful. Affirmations are a positive way to write a goal that you want to read daily and believe you can actually change your mindset to believe you can do it. If you truly practice this on a daily basis with an open mind and true desire, you can achieve a goal you have in place. Entrepreneurs, and many other successful athletes, sales and businesspeople have seen growth from changing the way they think and applying tools to change into a positive train of thoughts. In order for a affirmation to work properly, you have to only think positive. If a negative thought comes to mind, get rid of it or come back to the affirmation a few minutes later. Or write the positive version of that negative thought.

All affirmations need to be in the present; speak as it is happening right now. You see above how mine was written, but an example of one is: *I will inspire someone to write a book.* Another example: *I am determined to help people realize they are capable of achieving their goals.* Make your affirmations short and simple. Make sure you write everyone one as I or My. Lastly, for the first week, write your affirmations out five times a day with whatever hand you normally write with and one time a day with the opposite hand no matter how messy it is. I am right-handed, and when I write with my left hand, you can barely read any of the words. But by writing with the other hand, you are making your mind think in a different way.

You can also do this opposite hand if you are angry with someone. You can write them a letter with the other hand, so your brain thinks of the situation differently.

Then just tear up the letter. You do not need to give it to them, but it makes you see the situation in a different light.

Another thing I do that is similar to an affirmation is a WIN list every single day. I write my goals and to-do list on a daily basis. Each night, I highlight what wins I achieved, big or little; it does not matter. What marking the wins does for you is help you see that things are being accomplished, Helps keep you positive and on track daily. Life takes small steps to get there. I recently saw a picture of two ladders; one had little steps, and the person was almost to the top, and the other one was big steps, and the person could not start climbing them. That really resonated with me. You have to start at the bottom and work your way up to achieve success.

I have broken through so many barriers and gained so much confidence thanks to the support of this amazing community. This experience has given me hope. This hope and my newfound confidence are what got me where

I am now. And my new goal is hope—Hope-Help Other People Each Day. I got the courage to speak my story in a clubhouse room, which changed my life even more, and I found so many more people offering to help me along this journey. Words cannot express my gratitude, but none of it would have happened if I did not do a mindset shift and realize I can achieve it. I just need to go do it. I have made my goals and visions bigger than I thought were possible. It's because I have been given the gift to realize I am worthy, and I really hope this book makes you see that you are worthy too. I know you can find your worth within yourself if you stop worrying about what judgmental people think of you. Most are actually jealous, and it's their way of trying to make themselves look better. If you still don't believe you are strong enough to make a change within yourself, go listen to a podcast from Natasha Grano. She has a way of taking people under her wing with such a powerful presence. She helped me find my purpose.

I hope reading this book gives you confidence as you carry out your daily tasks. Anytime self-doubt starts to creep in, think, "If the True Airhead can do this with part of her brain missing, I can do it with a full brain!"

If the True Airhead can live a laptop lifestyle with part of her brain missing, you can live a laptop lifestyle with a full brain. If I can write a book with bad spelling and grammar, I know anyone reading this can write a book too. It's your choice to create the confidence within you. If you want to fly and follow your dreams, go for it.

If you ever start to doubt yourself or get those insecure feelings in your head, just come back and read this last three chapters and remember, I wrote this book with part of my brain missing, and I know you can do anything you want to achieve with a full brain!

You can do it to. I know you can!
Tammy Revard, The True Airhead

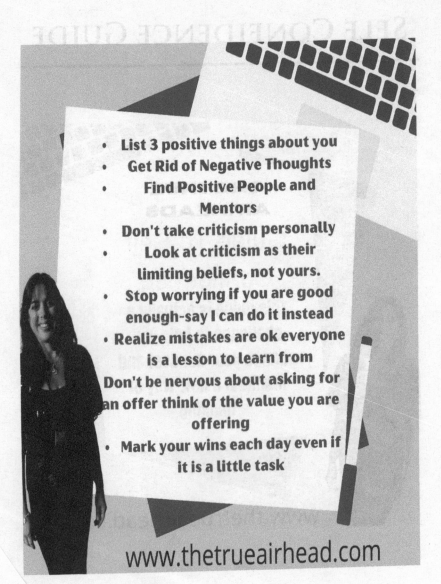

- List 3 positive things about you
- Get Rid of Negative Thoughts
- Find Positive People and Mentors
- Don't take criticism personally
- Look at criticism as their limiting beliefs, not yours.
- Stop worrying if you are good enough-say I can do it instead
- Realize mistakes are ok everyone is a lesson to learn from
- Don't be nervous about asking for an offer think of the value you are offering
- Mark your wins each day even if it is a little task

www.thetrueairhead.com

- List 30 things that bring you joy
- Go leave a $1 item at an elderly neighbors door with a note saying you care.
- Leave a note at someone's door who is struggling
- call a friend you have not talked to in a long time and just say hi.
- Find 25 things to do that do not cost money. Like a walk in the park as your walking think positive thoughts. If you think Negative turn around and walk a different way. Work your way to a Positive path when you go on that walk.

www.thetrueairhead.com

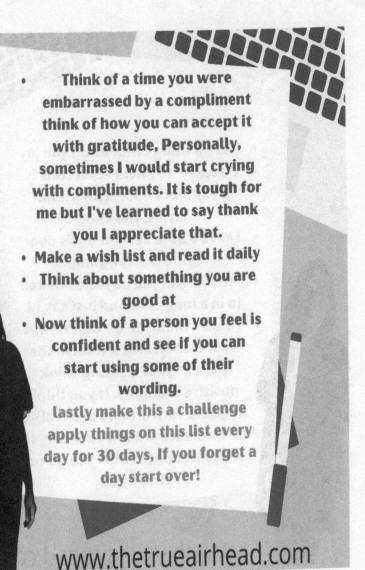

- Think of a time you were embarrassed by a compliment think of how you can accept it with gratitude, Personally, sometimes I would start crying with compliments. It is tough for me but I've learned to say thank you I appreciate that.
- Make a wish list and read it daily
- Think about something you are good at
- Now think of a person you feel is confident and see if you can start using some of their wording.

lastly make this a challenge apply things on this list every day for 30 days, If you forget a day start over!

www.thetrueairhead.com